Praise for
Inflection Point

"Scott Stawski weaves together a compelling set of observations regarding the technology 'perfect storm' that is gathering force and threatens to disrupt many businesses. By remaining centered on his own first-hand experiences and the thought leaders who have influenced him throughout his career, he crafts an entertaining and engaging story to demystify a complex subject. The result is a must-read for C-Suite executives looking to chart their own course through the current technology headwinds and to navigate successfully through their inflection point."

—Dave Sutton, Founder and CEO of TopRight Partners and coauthor of *Enterprise Marketing Management*

"Batten down the hatches! The IT department is under assault from the most unlikely of sources: one of its key suppliers. In a compelling book, Scott Stawski of Hewlett Packard predicts that the IT department of the future will buy no hardware or software and will shrink to a fraction of its current size. In its place, IT will become a broker of services supplied from the cloud. It's hard to argue with the powerful message of this well-written book."

—Al Ries, Chairman at Ries & Ries and best-selling author of *Positioning: The Battle for Your Mind*

"A timely reminder of the essential aspects of world class organizations and of how revolutionary technology changes will dictate future success."

—Gary Tessitore, CEO of Polyair Inter Pack Inc., Toronto, Canada

"Scott Stawski has methodically looked at technology and has a clear vision on how it will evolve in the future. Every CEO should read this book as he is on point about how technology is rapidly changing in today's business climate."

—Tammy O'Connor, former CEO, Red River Solutions

"This book is an eye-opener for CEOs and CIOs, and also for stakeholders and business technologists in general. The Continual Transformation Ecosystem operating model is the only way to go. If you think your business is at the verge of a technology-driven inflection point, you must read this book carefully. And if you don't think so, perhaps you should look around and think twice."

—Miguel Pereira, CEO, SocialNoise, a digital creative agency of reference in Spain and Mexico

"Scott Stawski delivers, in an engaging and easy-to-understand way, a clear vision of a connected future, accelerated disruption across industry, and how businesses can navigate the continual and rapid change."

—Scott Etkin, writer, journalist, and editor of *Data Informed*

"*Inflection Point* is an essential primer no matter what sort of business you are. Large incumbent? Quickly spot the weaknesses in your information infrastructure. Insurgent start-up? Map out where you can swiftly beat the established players. Three hours with this book will save you three years of pain."

—John V. Willshire, President, Smithery.co

Inflection Point

How the Convergence of Cloud, Mobility, Apps, and Data Will Shape the Future of Business

Scott Stawski

Executive, Hewlett Packard Enterprise

Publisher: Paul Boger
Editor-in-Chief: Amy Neidlinger
Executive Editor: Jeanne Glasser Levine
Development Editor: Natasha Wolmers
Editorial Assistant: Kristen Watterson
Cover Designer: Alan Clements
Managing Editor: Kristy Hart
Project Editor: Elaine Wiley
Copy Editor: Kitty Wilson
Proofreader: Katie Matejka
Indexer: Tim Wright
Senior Compositor: Gloria Schurick
Manufacturing Buyer: Dan Uhrig

© 2016 by Scott Stawski
Publishing as Pearson
Upper Saddle River, New Jersey 07458

For information about buying this title in bulk quantities, or for special sales opportunities (which may include electronic versions; custom cover designs; and content particular to your business, training goals, marketing focus, or branding interests), please contact our corporate sales department at corpsales@pearsoned.com or (800) 382-3419.

For government sales inquiries, please contact governmentsales@pearsoned.com.

For questions about sales outside the U.S., please contact international@pearsoned.com.

Company and product names mentioned herein are the trademarks or registered trademarks of their respective owners.

Printed in the United States of America

First Printing September 2015

ISBN-10: 0-13-438704-X
ISBN-13: 978-0-13-438704-8

Pearson Education LTD.
Pearson Education Australia PTY, Limited
Pearson Education Singapore, Pte. Ltd.
Pearson Education Asia, Ltd.
Pearson Education Canada, Ltd.
Pearson Educación de Mexico, S.A. de C.V.
Pearson Education—Japan
Pearson Education Malaysia, Pte. Ltd.

Library of Congress Control Number: 2015944611

Dedicated to my family.
For Mom and Dad,
who gave me the foundation for
the man I am today.

And for Hope, Henry, and Sun-Tzu,
who give me endless love daily.

Table of Contents

Foreword

We are in the midst of a major market disruption. Cloud, mobility, big data, and security are converging, and how enterprises respond will determine success or failure. Turning game-changing ideas into value faster than competitors is no longer a nice goal to have—it is the only way to survive and thrive. Companies like Uber and Airbnb didn't exist until a year or two ago, and they are already transforming their respective industries. We no longer have the luxury of time. We need to drive continuous transformation in our enterprise at the pace being set by these market-making competitors and radically shift to the way customers want to do business, or we risk losing them.

All of this is creating a true inflection point for executives around the world—disrupt or be disrupted. Companies need to embrace their core competencies and both act and react instantly to new strategies, tactics, and market pressures to ensure competitive advantage. In this book, Stawski uses real-life examples to demonstrate this need to drive continuous change and innovation, create new business models, and make technology a true business enabler.

This is an excellent guide for any CEO, CIO, and business or IT professional that is seeking to understand the changing world of enterprise IT, its relationship to a company's overall business strategy and success, and how to turn it into a competitive weapon that helps propel your business further, faster.

—Mike Nefkens, Executive Vice President, Enterprise Services, Hewlett Packard Enterprise

Acknowledgments

Ernest Hemingway once said, "There is nothing to writing. All you do is sit down at a typewriter and bleed." Well, I can now say from experience that he was correct. As the thesis began to shape in my mind, my original timeline for writing this book was 60 days. Surely, if I worked each and every weekend and many nights after the family fell asleep, I could have this book finished in two months. More than a year later, as I finish the final edits, I realize that even in one year, this book could not have been completed without the background, direct assistance, and overall motivation provided by many others.

I've dedicated this book to my mother, father, wife, son, and, yes, our dog Sun-Tzu. The foundation they have provided me in my life placed me at the keyboard. However, my wife Hope Stawski deserves special mention for her direct contributions to the project. Without her research, copy suggestions, copy edits, pictures, storytelling, and many late-night snacks, this book would not have been possible.

At the foundation of the thesis of this book are the concepts of core competency and competitive advantage—concepts discovered over the years in many different channels and venues, as well as in practical use. All of us using these concepts must acknowledge and thank C. K. Prahalad and Gary Hamel, who introduced the idea of "core competencies" nearly twenty-five years ago, in a *Harvard Business Review* article titled "The Core Competence of the Corporation." Their lifetime work around the concept of core competencies has influenced countless business leaders worldwide. We must also acknowledge and give thanks to Harvard Business School professor Michael Porter, who is an authority on competitive strategy and the author of *Competitive Advantage*. His theories on corporate strategy and competitive advantage are in use in C-level suites and board rooms around the world. This book and the thesis it puts forth would not be possible without the seminal works of those individuals.

I must extend heartfelt thanks to all the individuals at Pearson that made this book possible. Their encouragement and counsel has been invaluable. In particular, this book would not have been possible without the hard work of Jeanne Levine, Elaine Wiley, and Kitty Wilson. You made this happen, and I thank you.

Finally, I would like to thank all my colleagues at Hewlett Packard. While the thesis put forth in this book is solely my own and may not represent the views and/or opinions of Hewlett Packard, the nine years of employment with Hewlett Packard have afforded me an extraordinary opportunity to work with some of the best technologists, business consultants, and business operators in the world. In particular, I would like to give thanks to the support provided by Mike Nefkens, Louanne Buckley, Eric Harmon, Chris Donato, James Best, Laura Farmer, and Terence Ngai. From these individuals, I have learned and continue to learn. HP truly does make it matter every day.

About the Author

Scott Stawski is an Executive and Global Area Sales Leader for Hewlett Packard Enterprise. Scott is responsible for managing the sales and revenue generation activities for HP's largest and most strategic global accounts, exceeding $500M in revenue annually.

Prior to his current role, Scott oversaw the Applications Sales Group for the Americas at Hewlett Packard, including the automotive, manufacturing, industrial, energy, communication, media, and entertainment sectors. Over the preceding five years, Scott and his team have sold more than $3 billion in IT services.

Prior to executive-level sales leadership positions, Scott was in IT services delivery and account management. Scott brings a wealth of experience in business outcome-based technology service delivery. He has led numerous multimillion-dollar business intelligence and technology solutions and strategy engagements for Global 500 companies within the health and life science; manufacturing and technology; retail; travel; communication, media, and entertainment; and consumer packaged goods sectors.

Prior to joining Hewlett Packard, Scott was a Senior Principal at Knightsbridge, a leading business intelligence consultancy acquired by Hewlett Packard, where he developed business intelligence strategies and platforms for Fortune 500 companies.

Before entering technology consulting, Scott held executive and management positions at the CRM consultancy Inforte and newspaper chain Knight Ridder.

A trusted advisor for CEOs, CFOs, and CIOs in the Americas, Scott is a recognized expert in analytics and data management, technology strategy, outsourcing, and next-generation application transformation to the cloud. A contributing writer for leading publications, Scott is a speaker and facilitator at many of the leading industry shows and conferences and is frequently interviewed and quoted by leading media outlets, including *The Economist, The Chicago Tribune, San Francisco Chronicle, Editor & Publisher, Crain's Chicago Business*, and *National Public Radio*.

Scott is also Secretary of the Board for the Celina Economic Development Council and active with ChildFund International and Shakespeare Dallas and is working towards his Master of Liberal Arts, Extension Studies at Harvard University.

1

Introduction

Strategy needn't be mysterious. Conceptually, it is simple and straightforward. It requires clear and hard thinking, real creativity, courage, and personal leadership.

—A.G. Lafley, CEO, Procter & Gamble

When you think about going sailing off the coast of a faraway land, you probably don't imagine yourself fighting for your life in a sudden, horrible storm. But that's what happened to us, and I'm very fortunate to be alive to tell the tale.

Several years ago, I took a break from my responsibilities with Hewlett Packard Enterprise. I sailed with my wife, Hope, and my then-eight-year-old son, Henry, to St. Vincent and the Grenadines, a set of islands in the Lesser Antilles archipelago just north of Venezuela. As a family, we prefer deserted islands and hidden bays where we can drop anchor and let tranquility envelop us, as you can see in Figure 1-1.

Figure 1-1 The Stawski family, during a sailing trip to St. Vincent and the Grenadines.

We had been on vacation for fourteen days, sailing, snorkeling, and scuba diving while living on a fifty-foot ship named the *SS Angel in Paradise*. I was the captain, Hope was my executive officer, and Henry was the first mate. I had been around boats since I was a child, growing up near Chesapeake Bay, and I learned to sail when I was a student at the College of William and Mary. I passed on what I knew to my "crew." I taught them both seamanship, and they quickly became good sailors.

I am very careful when I am on the ocean. I have backup equipment, and I have backups for my backups—multiple GPS units, radios, and compasses. I always keep a "ditch bag" filled with food, water, a desalination system for getting drinkable water from the ocean, and another GPS and radio. In an emergency situation, the ditch bag is always ready to be tossed into a lifeboat or overboard.

During this trip, I checked the weather regularly, not just for the upcoming day but for the whole week. In the Caribbean, small "tropical squalls" tend to appear around three or four o'clock each afternoon. The seas leap around three to five feet, winds jump to twenty miles per hour, and rain falls for a time. This type of squall typically lasts an hour. If you're an experienced sailor, these squalls aren't a big deal. But on this particular day, I listened to the weather forecast and discovered that our expected tropical squall would be turning quickly into a full-blown tropical storm. Later, that same storm would continue to develop into Hurricane Alex, the first hurricane of the season.

At the time, we were about seventy-five miles off the coast of Bequia, nearly six hours from land.

We could see the storm coming, as shown in Figure 1-2. The boat's barometer plunged, the clouds darkened, the waves swelled, and the distance between the crests of the waves—their "wavelength"—compacted from a gentle 300 feet down to 50 feet; they hammered into our boat relentlessly. The winds worked their way up to a steady forty miles per hour, with gusts in the sixties. It was bad.

Figure 1-2 A normal squall turns into Tropical Storm and eventually Hurricane Alex.

I needed to project confidence for Hope and Henry while still providing the honest information they needed to hear. I told them that we were in some danger, and they could see that for themselves: it was already the worst storm they had ever seen at sea. I asked them to put on their full storm suits with their life jackets and then to harness themselves to the boat's lifelines, and I did the same while I helmed the ship. Hope double-checked the ditch bag to ensure that it was ready and sealed. We readied both the dinghy for possible use and the emergency lifeboat stowed under the transom of the boat.

When the storm hit with all its fury, Hope and I made eye contact. It was one of those nonverbal conversations spouses are able to have when they've been married for a long time: we didn't want Henry to panic. The wind speed had increased from forty to sixty miles per hour, with gusts now in the eighties. Wave height was now fifteen to twenty feet. We were under a small storm jib, which allowed us to keep the bow of the boat into the waves to prevent a knockdown. However, in storms like this, rogue waves tend to form. A rogue wave comes out of nowhere. It is bigger than the other waves and usually not traveling in the same direction as the regular waves. Several rogue waves hit us, the highest around twenty-five feet. We never capsized, but several times we experienced what in sailing lingo is known as a *knockdown*: the boat was pushed sideways to where the mast hits the water and pops back up.

This is when I fell in love with my wife all over again. As we rode out the storm, Hope started singing the theme to the old television show *Gilligan's Island*. It was hard to hear over the wild winds, but somehow the song calmed us, and we knew we would survive.

We rode out Tropical Storm Alex. It took about an hour and a half to get through the major part of the storm. After it passed, we experienced the calmest and most beautiful weather of the trip. We sailed on to a beautiful island called Mustique. We were exhausted and soaked, but we felt great about ourselves because we knew we had faced a daunting situation and prevailed.

It may seem like a cliché to compare business trends to stormy seas or to equate the responsibilities of CEOs to the job of a ship's captain, but after my experience in the Caribbean, these analogies took on new power for me. The parallel is completely apt. Trends in business are like the weather. Sometimes the world is calm and everything is smooth sailing. Sometimes a slight disturbance comes along, in the form of a squall or a new competitor. Sometimes squalls develop into full-blown storms—think declining profits or market share. Every now and then, a real life-or-death hurricane-like situation arises, wreaks terrible damage, and threatens to sink the whole proverbial ship.

As a consultant, I see these patterns over and over again at various companies. Businesses often sail headlong into "hurricanes," or what Andy Grove, the former CEO of Intel, calls *inflection points*—events that change the way we think and act. In Grove's book *Only the Paranoid Survive: How to Exploit the Crisis Points That Challenge Every Company,* he further elaborated that an *inflection point* is an event or a series of interrelated events that result in a significant change in the progress of a company, an industry, a sector, an economy, or even a nation. Inflection points can result from action taken by a company or from action taken by another entity that has a direct impact on that company. Regulatory changes, for instance, can lead to inflection points for companies by either introducing or removing constraints on the way those companies do business. In technology, the mainframes and the Internet have both created inflection points; in politics, the fall of the Berlin Wall and the assassination of John F. Kennedy were both events that became inflection points.

Grove was an immigrant moving to the United States from Hungary when he was twenty years old. He is a true pioneer of Silicon Valley and an icon in the semiconductor industry. Grove never forgot the history that brought him to America, nor the upheavals that began to shape his thinking. In his memoir, *Swimming Across: A Memoir*, Grove writes:

I had lived through a Hungarian fascist dictatorship, German military occupation, the Nazis' "Final Solution," the siege of Budapest by the Soviet Red Army, a period of chaotic democracy in the years immediately after the war, a variety of repressive Communist regimes, and a popular uprising that was put down at gunpoint...[during the course of which] many young people were killed [and] countless others were interned. Some two hundred thousand Hungarians escaped to the West. I was one of them.

Later in life, his deeply personal experience with trends, upheavals, actions, reactions, and business storms began to take shape. Of particular interest to Grove was how to recognize when a business or business leader became immersed in a trend that was really something more—an inflection point. "New rules prevailed now—and they were powerful enough to force us into actions that cost us nearly half a billion dollars. The trouble was, not only didn't we realize that the rules had changed—what was worse, we didn't know what rules we now had to abide by."

History shows that, when businesses come upon inflection points, most take cautious steps that are too small and insignificant to address the change. Laggards who underestimate the change or misunderstand the real nature of it do too little—and pay the price by going out of business. Eastern Airlines, RCA, Woolworth Company, and Circuit City are just a few examples of companies that have failed to weather their industries' inflection points. Yet, for each inflection point, there are also always businesses that understand the opportunity and seize it; they move first, and they reap the rewards. So, for every Borders and Blockbuster that goes out of business, there is an Amazon that not only took their place but probably caused the disruption that resulted in their demise.

The business world today is changing very quickly; we are in the midst of a major inflection point that is leading to a host of changes—a lot of stormy weather. Companies that can understand and predict the impact of these changes have the opportunity to leverage them for true competitive advantage.

This new, major inflection point for business is a combination of several trends that together are causing major business disruption. At the foundation of this inflection point is information technology, specifically the convergence of cloud, mobility, software as a service (SaaS), and data. It is this convergence that is powering a second and more significant round of disintermediation and in some cases reintermediation under new business models.

We will discuss and define disintermediation, reintermediation, and the resulting business disruption in the next chapter. That being said, with every business disruption, there is a potential opportunity. Companies can use the same technology convergence that is powering today's inflection point not only to survive but to thrive. This is what Hewlett Packard Enterprise calls "The New Style of IT"—a complete reshaping of how businesses use information technologies.

For the past forty years, IT has been transforming the business world by devising new processes for production, operations, and personal productivity, and by revolutionizing the ways in which people communicate and collaborate. IT was at the forefront of our culture's last major inflection point—mainstream use of the Internet—and now it is pushing forward an array of new, game-changing ideas: cloud technologies, mobility, SaaS, and Big Data. As these technologies converge and become "consumerized," operational IT will slip into the background of all business activities and become both a utility and a true business enabler—empowering companies to focus on their core competency and power an operating model that embraces speed and flexibility through continual transformation.

The "new style of IT" promises greater simplicity, agility, speed, and affordability. IT as a real business utility is here now, and its presence means that no company should ever have to "buy" a software license or "own" a piece of IT hardware again.

A handful of young companies have already grasped this new reality: Netflix, Uber, and Snapchat have all become household names by embracing a new technology operating model. But other companies are continuing to spend way too much on outdated operational IT. *CIO* magazine, which conducts an annual "State of the CIO" survey, found in 2013 that the average IT budget as a percentage of revenue was 5.2 percent, up from 4.7 percent the year before. Gartner Research said that 80 percent of enterprises would overspend on IT through 2014. NPI Research estimated that companies overspent by more than $207 billion on technology and telecom purchases in 2010 alone—and that number is increasing.

From my personal experience examining many companies, I estimate that enterprises are overspending on IT by as much as 40 percent. Every dollar they spend on operational IT is non-revenue-generating and comes directly out of their profit margins. And the traditional capital expenditure (CAPEX) IT they are purchasing is locking their businesses into an inflexible operating model that is hurting their competitive advantage.

This overspending is especially surprising because the business professionals who are making these decisions are already behaving like savvy consumers in their home and personal lives—just not in their businesses. As consumers, we don't care where our electricity comes from—wind, solar, nuclear, whatever: we flip a switch, and we get light. Similarly, if we want a social media platform to connect us to our family and friends, we hit a button on our smartphone, and we're connected. We do the same for each of the IT tasks in our personal lives: e-mail, personal accounting, our daily calendar, video meetings, and chatting. This is the consumerization of IT.

But in business, these same basic tasks are thought to require a great deal of customized IT work, with a tremendous amount of IT department interface and CAPEX. There hasn't been a consumerization of IT as a utility in the business world. The objective of most current IT departments is still to "build and run." They build IT, and they run IT. In the future, however, the objective of the IT department will be not to build or run anything at all but to be a service broker of IT business enablers. They will establish an architecture, set standards, and provide governance for an ecosystem of providers that supply the IT services to their business users.

Penguin Corporation Deals with IT

Let's look at a hypothetical large, old-line company that I'll call "Penguin Corp." Penguin is a global consumer packaged goods company headquartered on the West Coast that is struggling to make decisions about its IT future. The company uses Microsoft Office, which employees download, and Microsoft Outlook, which employees use to access e-mail and is hosted on the company's computers in data centers throughout the world. It has twenty data centers located throughout the world that it either owns or leases. Penguin has hundreds of enterprise applications from software companies such as SAP, Oracle, and Microsoft, from which it purchased licenses and pays annual software maintenance fees to run on servers in those data centers.

Penguin has more than 40,000 employees, and it purchases tablets, laptops, or workstations for most of those employees. This company generates $35 billion in worldwide revenue and spends 4 percent—or $1.4 billion a year—on operational IT. It spends an additional $140 million on IT capital expenditures. Only the depreciation of that expense is included in the $1.4 billion number cited above. So, Penguin Corp's real IT cash outlay is closer to $1.54 billion annually. The CEO and CFO have benchmarked their IT expenditures. The

Fortune 500 IT spend is slightly above 4 percent of gross revenue and the overall median is 3 to 5 percent, so everyone at Penguin is comfortable with the current IT budget.

Upper management recognizes that the world is moving away from these localized software installations and moving toward the cloud. So, their major initiative this year will be switching the whole company from Microsoft Office 2010 to Microsoft Office 365. Office 365 is delivered to users through the cloud and includes Exchange Online for email, SharePoint Online for collaboration, Lync Online for chat and other communications, and a suite of Office apps— web-based versions of the traditional Microsoft Office suite of applications. This cloud-based package will free Penguin from needing to install and run any of this software through its own data centers.

This is Penguin's major transformation initiative for the year. Penguin is looking to address the trend toward cloud computing by making an incremental decision—not a transformative one. It may be addressing the trend, but it is not getting ahead of it. What would a transformative scenario look like for Penguin? It would involve eliminating all data centers, moving 90 percent of all application workloads to the cloud, rationalizing and reducing the application footprint by 40 percent, and moving all applications to consumption-based SaaS, with a significant open-source application footprint. How about reducing the overall IT spend by 30 percent and reducing capital expenditures by 95 percent?

Why would a well-run profitable company decide to make small, incremental changes when transformative ones are required? There are a variety of reasons. Organizations tend to prefer incremental change to transformational change. Penguin's management believes they should keep their legacy applications because their employees are comfortable with them. They're convinced that it's too difficult to initiate a more transformational change at a big company. And Penguin's CIO, like his counterparts at other major companies, may have tunnel vision when it comes to keeping IT assets under direct ownership. CIOs like to develop technology. True, every CIO wants to meet the needs of his or her company's business users. In the old IT model, that meant building, owning, and running every aspect of the IT department. This led to the building of IT empires with a lot of people working for them, and the old model ensured the value of these people within the company.

In general, CEOs and CFOs seldom disregard the recommendations they receive from their CIOs—largely because they lack the background to do so. CFOs by function come from finance. CEOs usually come from finance, marketing, or sales. Rarely do we see a CEO with an IT background, so when the CIO tells a CEO something about a trend in technology, the CEO tends to accept rather than question deeply.

So, in the case of Penguin, the company will invest in an incremental solution that gives the false impression that the company is not falling too far behind the curve. In the short run, it will continue to be profitable and a leader in their industry. But over time, the ongoing, unnecessary commitment of energy and resources to IT will interfere with the company's ability to think creatively, innovate, and establish a continual transformation environment (CTE). In short, in today's business environment, Penguin will lose competitive advantage.

Today, we are at the next major set of inflection points. Massive business disruption is occurring, and this disruption is accelerating and becoming more impactful. At the same time, the convergence of trends in cloud, mobility, SaaS, and Big Data can dramatically change the operational IT landscape for businesses. For operational IT, companies must move to a consumption-based utility environment powered by business-user selection of the technology enablers and business process providers necessary to best perform their functions. The IT department of today must transform into a brokerage of these IT services, with functions and processes outside the company's core competency handled by an ecosystem of trusted partners and providers.

Market pressure and business disruption from the current inflection points are only going to increase. However, as CIOs and enterprises embrace this new style of IT, management bandwidth and operating and capital expenditures will be freed to allow companies to focus on their core competencies. And this consumption-based, IT-as-a-utility ecosystem will provide the flexibility and scalability to create a CTE that will power competitive advantage strategies.

Understanding Operational IT Versus Product Development IT: What Is the Difference?

The thesis of this book involves a fundamental change in the way operational IT is provided to the business users of a company by the IT department. To understand this imperative, we must also understand that we are discussing operational IT only. Operational IT is the IT enablers necessary to run the business operations of a company. IT enablers are needed for sales, administration, marketing, finance, operations, human resources, and manufacturing and distribution. Operational IT is not a product or service that the company takes to market; rather, it is what enables the business's functional areas. It is this operational IT for which companies must change the current operating model to the "new style of IT."

IT is the product or service of some companies. For software companies, product development IT (also known as just plain R&D) is synonymous with product innovation. Product development IT is at the heart of the products or services offered by web-based service companies like Facebook. These companies require product development IT, and that development is intimately tied to their core competencies. While these companies should also move their operational IT to the new style of IT, they must continue to nourish their product development IT as a key internal business unit within the company. In fact, moving the operational IT to the new business model will free up resources and management bandwidth to broaden and deepen the R&D/product development functions for these companies.

2

The Storm on the Horizon

Our intuition about the future is linear. But the reality of information technology is exponential, and that makes a profound difference. If I take thirty steps linearly, I get to thirty. If I take thirty steps exponentially, I get to a billion.

—Ray Kurzweil, author, inventor, and futurist

My wife and I bought an older convertible for our son Henry when he turned sixteen—a typical American rite of passage. Almost immediately, one of the plastic emblems fell off the front wheel. My son, being part of a generation whose smartphones are always planted firmly in their hands, went into action. He took a picture of the plastic emblem from the other front tire. An app using visual recognition technology immediately identified the part and provided an online store where it was sold. The app sent the link to the store and the exact part number to his phone via text. He then called me to explain what had happened.

Being the understanding dad that I am, I told him to forward me the text with the link for the replacement. I clicked on the link, clicked Purchase, and clicked on Google Wallet for instant payment. The entire scenario unfolded in less than ten minutes. The part arrived at our house two days later. It fit and matched perfectly.

When I was Henry's age, I had an old car, too. When it needed attention, my dad and I had to drive to a vintage car store (i.e., a junk-yard). We needed the clerk's help to search high and low through old, dirty boxes for our obscure part or bolt, and then, if we found it—and there was never a guarantee that we would—my dad had to write a check or hand over some of the cash he'd remembered to withdraw from the bank before it closed for the weekend. Several weeks would inevitably pass before all the stars and planets aligned to actually find, purchase, and install the part. Ah, the old days.

This story illustrates several trends that are converging to create a major storm—or inflection point—today.

What Is the Difference between Trend and Inflection Point?

At the Academy of Management's annual meeting several years ago, Andy Grove expounded on his concept of inflection points. After sketching out his theory, he admitted that inflection points "almost always hit the corporation in such a way that those of us in senior management are among the last ones to notice." He warned that "depending on the actions you take in responding to this challenge, you will either go on to new heights or head downward in your prosperity as a firm."

Grove went on to say that the biggest difficulty with inflection points is distinguishing these major turning points from any of the other various changes that regularly confront a business. He asked, "How do you know if a change is just a garden-variety change or qualifies to be this monumental, catastrophic change category that we call an 'inflection point'?" He said that he hasn't yet come up with a satisfactory answer to that question, but he believes there are some key warning signs that a company is facing an inflection point:

When it is clear to you that, all of a sudden, the company or the entity that you worry about has shifted. You have dealt with one particular company or establishment as a competitor all your life, and all of a sudden, you don't care about them. You care about what somebody else thinks. I have this mental silver bullet test: "If you have one bullet, who would you shoot with it?" If you change the direction of the gun, that is one of the signals that you may be dealing with something more than an ordinary shift in the competitive landscape.

Another warning sign:

When people who you worked with for twenty years, who you have a lot of respect for, who normally nobody is talking about, and then suddenly everybody seems to talk about them—it's time to sit up and listen and to see what's going on.

As an example, Grove reminded his audience of what happened when Amazon began competing with Barnes & Noble. In two short years, the upstart online retailer managed to eclipse Barnes & Noble not only in sales but also in market valuation. In fact, Amazon's market value was bigger than that of Barnes & Noble and their next biggest competitor, Borders, Inc. (now out of business) combined.

In hindsight, this was clearly an inflection point for Barnes & Noble, and only time will tell whether that company can survive it. Most other major bookstore chains are now out of business, including Borders, Waldenbooks, Brentano's, Crown Books, and B. Dalton.

Grove proposes several ways companies can identify inflection points. One is to make empirical observations of any growing divergence between a company's strategic statements and its strategic actions. In Grove's opinion, management needs to focus on the company's strategic actions because "strategic actions are driven by the competition, driven by the sales force, driven by the sheer necessity of winning business in the marketplace day in and day out."

Second, Grove says to take care in assessing data: "I'm going to say you have to argue with the data at times like this, because the data that deals with your business are pertinent to your past, and don't say anything about your future."

Third, he says, "It is extremely important to be able to listen to the people who bring you bad news—who are typically lower-level people."

The major business storm approaching, the inflection point that is here today, will be stronger—and the change faster—than most companies anticipate. Technological advances will continue to change business and the social fabric of our society, but the rate of change will increase exponentially. What needs to be emphasized and clearly understood is that the rate of change is changing. Practical examples are now coming to light daily. The list of industry sectors that have disappeared or severely contracted continues to grow, and the disruption that used to take place over multiple decades—as happened with wired telecommunications, for example—can now happen within a single decade (e.g., book distribution, travel), or within less than half a decade (e.g., music distribution, insurance), or within a couple years (e.g., video rental, client/server software and licensing). In some industries, such as product prototyping and the taxicab industry, the rate of disruption now can be measured in months.

Companies like Polaroid, Kodak, and RadioShack either disappear or continue as shadows of their former selves, and others like Snapchat and Uber seem to appear everywhere overnight.

This is not the time for business as usual. This is not the time for incremental change. This inflection point requires ultimate business flexibility. In order to succeed, a company must be driven by its core competencies and powered by a continual transformation environment that allows it the flexibility to innovate and achieve competitive advantage in this dynamic environment.

Disintermediation Will Continue and Accelerate

One aspect of the business disruption that is occurring today is the phenomenon called *disintermediation*. Disintermediation is nothing more than the elimination of the middleman, and it has been sweeping our economy, eliminating vast segments of every industry's value and supply chain in its wake. Disintermediation is a major trend for businesses, and we can expect it to grow more widespread and accelerate in the years to come.

Disintermediation is the process by which intermediaries in a supply chain—distributors, wholesalers, brokers, or agents—are removed from that chain. Instead of dealing with these middlemen, the customer deals directly with the provider of the good or service— as when I ordered Henry's replacement car part. Disintermediation is made possible by a new high level of market transparency and buying convenience that lets consumers know the value of supply prices and pay less for items by buying directly and more conveniently from a manufacturer or some other disintermediary that has contracted the value chain. This is amusingly shown in Figure 2-1.

Figure 2-1 Disintermediation is increasing, and a further more impactful round of business disruption will occur. (Courtesy of Bryant Arnold, Cartoonaday.com)

The term *disintermediation* was coined and applied to the banking industry in the late 1960s. It referred to consumers who were investing directly in securities (stocks and government and private bonds) rather than leaving their money in savings accounts. It was also used to describe borrowers going to the capital markets rather than to banks. In short, borrowers took their business to the places their bank would have taken their business—just without involving the banks.

The term was later applied to cutting out the middleman in general commerce, though the original usage remained predominant. Only in the late 1990s, with the rise of the Internet, did the term and the idea behind it become widely popularized.

The impact of disintermediation has been enormous. Consider book and music stores, computer hardware and software, the distribution of movies, and travel agencies—all industries that have been turned inside out since the 1990s. Companies like Amazon, Netflix, and Apple have been revolutionizing the way we consume and establishing new expectations. If Jeff Bezos has his way (and he usually does), the skies will soon be filled with drones delivering packages from Amazon warehouses, with many of these products having been manufactured by Amazon.

Beyond the obvious companies such as Apple, Amazon, and Netflix, let's take a look at a few other companies that exemplify disintermediation.

Tesla

Tesla Motors initially gained widespread attention when it unveiled the Tesla Roadster, the first fully electric sports car. Production on the Roadster ended in 2012, and Tesla launched its second vehicle, the Model S, a fully electric luxury sedan. Though the Model S is priced at $100,000 (the Roadster cost a bit more), Tesla CEO Elon Musk says he sees Tesla as an independent automaker and that Tesla eventually intends to offer electric cars at prices that are affordable to the average consumer. Tesla hopes its current project, a vehicle that costs around $35,000, will be available by 2017.

The company is named after Nikola Tesla, a Serbian-American inventor, engineer, and futurist who once worked for Thomas Edison. Tesla is best known for his involvement with the design of the alternating current (AC) electricity delivery system we use today. Despite his many accomplishments, he fell into obscurity after his death in 1943. The Tesla Roadster's AC motor is a direct descendant of Nikola Tesla's original design from 1882.

A number of prominent entrepreneurs have invested in Tesla Motors, including Google cofounders Sergey Brin and Larry Page, former eBay president Jeff Skoll, Hyatt heir Nick Pritzker, and a number of prominent venture capital firms.

Unlike other major car manufacturers, Tesla sells its cars directly to consumers, without using car dealers as intermediaries. Tesla has stores and "galleries"—usually located in shopping malls—in twenty-two locations throughout the United States. Customers cannot purchase vehicles in these stores; instead, they order them on the Tesla Motors website. The galleries are located in states with more restrictive dealership protection laws that prohibit test drives and discussions about prices or financing, among other restrictions.

Tesla's strategy of owning its own stores and service centers and pursuing direct customer sales is a significant departure from the standard dealership model that has long dominated the US vehicle marketplace. Currently, twenty-eight states have laws that ban manufacturers from selling vehicles directly to consumers, and every single automaker except Tesla uses independently owned dealerships. Dealership associations in several states have filed suit against Tesla Motors because its new business model threatens the dealers' positions as supply-chain middlemen.

Texas currently has the strictest dealership protection laws in the United States. The state's requirement that all new cars be purchased through third-party dealerships effectively blocks Tesla from selling cars in Texas. A Texas resident may still buy from Tesla Motors, but the purchase must be handled as an out-of-state transaction.

The obstacles being thrown at Tesla show a frightened industry working to combat an inflection point at the exact moment when it should be embracing the change. The future of the auto industry will inevitably involve manufacturers selling directly to consumers. The natural end state of auto manufacturing is selling custom-made cars on demand, directly to consumers—and it is within our reach. Automotive dealerships as we know them today will eventually disappear. Tesla is just the first company to seize on the inflection point.

Shapeways

You may not have heard of Shapeways yet, but you will. Shapeways is the world's largest provider of 3-D printing, a service that is already having a significant impact on the prototype development market and is expected to become the largest disintermediation-based industry disrupter within the next few years.

To put it in simple terms, 3-D printing uses digital image files to create three-dimensional objects from "dust." These printers do not print pages, they print actual three dimensional objects. These objects can be simple (see Figure 2-2), or they can be fully functional, ready-to-use tools. I was amazed at a demonstration where a working adjustable wrench was "printed" in front of my eyes. This technology is improving rapidly. It is already possible to create simple tools with simple, movable parts, and soon it will be possible to create much more complex objects.

Figure 2-2 Shapeways is empowering a more powerful round of disintermediation. (Courtesy of Shapeways.)

The implications of this are far-reaching. The day will come when industrial companies will no longer need to keep millions of dollars' worth of replacement parts on hand but will be able to create them as needed with 3-D printers. Ordinary consumers will be able to "print" simple tools like screwdrivers at home rather than run out to a hardware store. Consider the emblem on the wheel of Henry's car, or my trips to the junkyard with my dad when I was Henry's age; these kinds of experiences may one day be relics of the past. We may be able to simply print the parts we need at home. There are already medical uses for this technology: for example, a surgeon can scan a patient's damaged knee and print out a replacement one on the spot. The day is not far off when even complex electronic devices like smartphones will be produced with this technology.

Shapeways, which is currently based in New York City, was founded in 2007 and launched in 2008 by CEO Peter Weijmarshausen, Robert Schouwenburg, and Marleen Vogelaar as a spin-off of a Dutch company called Royal Philips Electronics.

"Shapeways is the largest 3-D printing marketplace and community online," Weijmarshausen says. "We make it possible for anyone to use 3-D printers, so you do not need to physically own one."

Shapeways may be the ultimate example of disintermediation. They have eliminated the manufacturer, wholesaler, and retailer in the value chain. This is why the $2.2 billion market that existed for 3-D printing services in 2012 is expected to grow to $25 billion by 2020, which of course will disrupt many different industries. Indeed, it may even spark the next industrial revolution.

Orbitz

I was the practice lead for Communications, Media, and Entertainment and senior consultant at Braun Consulting when our firm began working with a startup called Orbitz. Orbitz began with the financial backing of four airlines and a business plan prepared by Boston Consulting Group. What it needed was a technology visionary, and it got that with Alex Zoghlin. Zoghlin was Orbitz's first employee and CTO. He was also a computer wizard and a pioneer in the development of web browsers when he worked with Netscape cofounder Marc Andreessen at the University of Illinois. (Andreessen would join the Orbitz board a couple years later, in 2003.) Zoghlin brought in Braun Consulting for its experience with data and analytics, and I was asked to lead several strategic technology work streams.

Orbitz Worldwide, Inc., operates a website consumers can use to make travel arrangements. Orbitz.com—the flagship brand of Orbitz Worldwide—began operating in 2001. Other Orbitz online travel companies include CheapTickets, ebookers (in Europe), HotelClub, and RatestoGo (based in Sydney, Australia). Orbitz Worldwide also owns and operates a corporate travel company called Orbitz for Business.

Orbitz was the air travel industry's response to the rise of travel-booking websites like Travelocity and Expedia, and a solution to lower airline distribution costs. Continental, Delta, Northwest, United Airlines, and American Airlines invested a combined $145 million to start the project in November 1999. It was code-named T2 (some wondered whether that stood for "Travelocity Terminator"), but when it commenced corporate operations as DUNC, LLC (the initials of its first four founding airlines) in February 2000, it was given the brand name Orbitz. These airlines needed to disintermediate the disintermediaries—Travelocity and Expedia. That is the pace of change necessary in today's world.

Orbitz.com's June 2001 launch was the most successful e-commerce launch in more than two years, beating the launches of Target.com and Walmart.com with more than two million visitors during its first month. (Orbitz Worldwide sites now generate that many visitors *every day*.) Little more than three years later, the Cendant Corporation bought Orbitz for $1.25 billion, making it part of the Cendant Travel Distribution Services Group division. In 2006, the Blackstone Group purchased the Travelport business, which included Orbitz, from Cendant. In February 2015, the consolidation of an industry totally disrupted by disintermediation continued when Expedia acquired Orbitz and Travelocity.

Orbitz's fanatical focus on analyzing user data to better serve customers started with Alex Zoghlin and continues today with Barney Harford, the forty-three-year-old CEO of Orbitz Worldwide. In order to achieve this focus, Harford first needed to get all the worldwide Orbitz companies onto a common technology platform—a project he completed early in 2012. While Orbitz is still a relatively young company, Harford understands that it is necessary to keep a continual transformation environment operating model in place in order to remain nimble.

The new unified platform allows Orbitz to innovate faster, more easily, and more cost-effectively by rolling out features across all Orbitz Worldwide properties. This unification has helped Orbitz respond quickly to advances in technology and changes in customer behavior. For example, the platform was able to adapt and accommodate the rapid growth of bookings on mobile devices like smartphones and tablets. Harford noted that Orbitz's iPhone app is the only online travel app to be inducted into Apple's App Store "Hall of Fame," and it's one of just forty-eight apps out of an ecosystem of seven hundred thousand to be honored in this way.

Where Travelocity was able to anticipate the disintermediation that would disrupt the travel industry, Orbitz was able to build on that idea and anticipate other inflection points, too—particularly the rise of mobile platforms and the rapid evolution of data analytics. In today's ever-changing environment, there will be rounds of disruption, disintermediation, reintermediation, and even post-disintermediation consolidation.

We know disintermediation is not a new topic. Again, Amazon, Apple, Travelocity, and many others have forever changed entire industries, affecting thousands of companies and hundreds of thousands of jobs.

But this is only the beginning. We are on the cusp of an even greater round of disintermediation. Faster than many companies think, we will see monumental shifts in the value and supply chains in healthcare, manufacturing, insurance, finance, and consumer packaged goods. Manufacturers, wholesalers, distributors, and other intermediaries will be eliminated. More and more companies will go to market directly to the consumer or through marketplaces that bypass traditional channels. Many well-known companies will cease to exist, and others will rise.

This accelerated change and accelerated business disruption are being powered by a truly connected world, a world where everything is collected and data recorded, a world of Big Data. This world is "the Internet of Everything"—and it is right around the corner. In the very near future, if an emblem were to fall off the car Henry was driving, the car itself would send a message to our home 3-D printer, which would output a replacement emblem and have it ready for Henry by the time he got home. We are on the verge of living in a thinking machine-to-machine world, one in which our devices and products themselves will anticipate and accommodate many of our needs, with little or no intervention from us.

How Will You Participate in the Internet of Everything?

The Internet of Everything (IoE), also known as the Internet of Things (IoT), is exponentially accelerating disintermediation. Billions of objects—mechanical devices like refrigerators, washers, air conditioners, and even industrial production machines—sense and predict users' needs and communicate and share information with one another automatically. These connected objects, as illustrated in Figure 2-3, then produce data, which is regularly collected, analyzed, and used to initiate action.

**THE INTERNET
OF EVERYTHING**

Figure 2-3 The IOE is on the verge of connecting literally everything.

This data provides business intelligence for logistics, planning, execution, and decision-making. Though the Internet of Everything is already a trillion-dollar industry, Cisco predicts that the trend will quickly grow even bigger: it estimates that there will be thirty-seven billion new Internet-connected devices by 2020. Consider that the human population projection for the same period is only slightly over eight billion. Data coming from inanimate objects will issue orders to replenish vending machines, replace cars' oil filters, and reroute trucks during transit. And, those trucks may be driverless. The data that will be produced, submitted, and analyzed will forever change all kinds of products—and our daily lives.

Recently, as part of its iOS8 operating system, Apple introduced a new framework called HomeKit, designed to communicate with household appliances. With HomeKit, iPhones can now lock doors, adjust lights, set alarms, and adjust household temperatures. Google's latest Android release has similar capabilities, allowing Android devices to communicate with one another automatically.

The Internet of Everything is set to change, well, everything. Let's take a look at some examples.

The Internet of Health

Already, many people are using wrist-worn fitness monitors such as the popular Fitbit to track how many steps they take in a day, how many miles they run, how many calories they burn, and even how well they are sleeping. Apple's HealthKit collects health-related data from wearable devices and enables users to share key information like heart rate and blood pressure with their doctors.

Proteus Digital Health, a pioneer of "smart pill" technology, has developed the Proteus service offering, which employs an ingestible sensor (see Figure 2-4). The Proteus offering helps patients monitor their health from the inside; it tells physicians and family members whether patients are taking their prescribed medications.

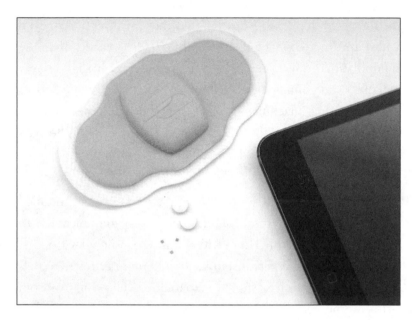

Figure 2-4 Proteus ingestible sensors is only one example of the Internet of Health.

Kolibree, a French company, has designed toothbrush sensors that calculate and rate how well people are brushing their teeth, their brushing style, and their thoroughness. After brushing, the user is given real-time feedback.

Recently, Intel introduced a new smart shirt that contains conductive fibers. The shirt tracks a wearer's heart-rate information and transmits it via Bluetooth to a computer or smartphone.

In Taiwan, a company known as AiO has designed smart clothing. The first application of this technology will be shirts to be worn by Taiwan's bus drivers. The shirts monitor drivers to sense whether they are falling asleep or whether their vital signs are dropping. The information the shirt provides is expected to reduce accident rates.

We have entered an era in which healthcare will become proactive rather than reactive, a change that will be driven by this availability of data for proactive analysis.

The Internet of Traffic

Hope, Henry, and I will soon be able to call a driverless car with the push of a button and have the car drive us to our destination. Google is well down the path of developing such a vehicle. Apple is rumored to be developing driverless technology as well. Along the way, this car will sense other vehicles and pedestrians in its path, determine the quickest route, and reroute whenever it senses an accident or a traffic jam. At the end of the trip, I will be billed automatically. This service—possibly only a few years away in some areas—will put severe pressure on the taxi industry: it is the ultimate "Uber" experience, and it will make traffic accidents—and the tragedies associated with them—a thing of the past.

The Internet of Retail and Consumer Packaged Goods

Retail stores are already capable of delivering highly personalized customer experiences through the smart use of consumer data. Thanks to the IoE, deep insights into consumer behavior combined with ever-improving predictive analysis will lead to better and better product offerings aimed directly at each specific customer.

Retailers are also using the Internet of Everything to optimize their inventory through automated replenishment processes based on real-time demand information, stock levels, and environmental factors: they know exactly what products they need and where, in real time.

More and more consumer-packaged goods companies will work with manufacturers to sense and automate replenishment. Why not have an automated detergent dispenser or replenishment for your GE washing machine (see Figure 2-5)? Why not have it sense when its supply is low and signal Amazon to automatically send Tide to the house in a subscription-based direct-to-consumer model?

Figure 2-5 Amazon is experimenting with physical "buy" buttons that can be placed in various locations throughout a consumer's home—in the kitchen, in a bathroom drawer, or even in a broom closet. These buttons can be used to order laundry detergent or other household necessities by syncing with the Amazon mobile app via the Wi-Fi network in the user's home. In a recent blog post, John V. Willshire of Smithery made an interesting point: "What brand would you nail to a wall with the same conviction that you'd put up a picture in your house?" (Courtesy of Smithery.co.)

The Internet of Assets

Smart devices and sensors will soon transform enterprise asset management and field service operations. Companies will be able to predict when machines or components are due for preventive maintenance, and they will be able to provide service and replace faulty parts *before* systems break down.

The Internet of Design

As "smart" products begin to proliferate, product development and life-cycle management will change at all points in the supply chain. Some companies may begin to build a more holistic digital product master by adding electronic components to traditionally mechanical products. R&D teams will equip products with sensors to collect service and performance data to improve analysis and simulation capabilities, which will enable them to continually improve the design and performance of their products based on automated consumer feedback.

The Internet of Manufacturing and Logistics

The emergence of machine-to-machine (M2M) and of the Internet of Everything are changing the operational environment of today's manufacturing firms. There are about one hundred million M2M devices. That number is expected to grow to over seven hundred million and lead to revenue of $88 billion by 2023 (up from $10 billion in 2013).

Businesses are using the Internet of Everything to reshape their supply chains by analyzing real-time data from shipping containers to make their logistics operations as efficient as possible. This real-time information from track-and-trace systems makes it possible for any company that depends on logistics to identify problems and resolve them immediately. Some feel that this inflection point in manufacturing constitutes a fourth industrial revolution.

Each industrial revolution that has significantly increased output has been driven by either a single technology or a convergence of technology enablers. Many anticipate the next revolution, the fourth industrial revolution (or Industry 4.0), to be driven by connectivity of everything.

This fourth industrial revolution has five characteristics that explain the direct impact of the connections between technological enablers on manufacturing processes:

- These embedded, interconnected devices are widely used.

- At every stage of the manufacturing process, smart devices provide raw data and feedback that can be used to automate and manage process-control systems.

- The proliferation of smart devices will cause control systems to become more complex and widespread.

- Wireless technology will link these distributed control modules and allow control system components to be dynamically reconfigured.

- The importance of actionable intelligence will increase due to the impossibility of anticipating all the environmental changes that control systems will need to respond to.

The Internet of Supply Chain

Through the use of smart technologies, goods may soon be transported without human intervention from manufacturers to suppliers (or directly to consumers). Warehouses will become completely automated: goods will move in and out without the need for employees to move them. Goods will be ordered and replenished using information provided by smart sensors that will be able to optimize transit routes. Replenishment requests will be sent to suppliers automatically, and those suppliers will be able to provide order status information. The dynamic production and transportation network created by all this automation will improve the efficiency of the entire supply chain.

In short, the supply chain will be radically transformed from what it was like even a few years ago. The Internet of Everything is coming, and this resultant inflection point will continue to demand that businesses adapt or die. It will be interesting to see how businesses respond. Which ones will reinvent themselves, and which ones will disappear?

These two trends—disintermediation and the Internet of Everything—are converging into a disruptive inflection point that should motivate every C-level executive to embrace change. Business executives have a unique opportunity now for reintermediation. They have a chance to reinsert their products and services into the value and supply chain in a way that recognizes the inflection points in the marketplace and gives them competitive advantage. Seizing this opportunity will make it possible for companies not only to survive the storm but also thrive. This requires a re-dedication to a fanatical focus on core competency, clear alignment with a competitive advantage strategy, and an operating model built on a continual transformation environment.

These requirements will be the topic of our next chapter.

How the New Style of IT Thwarts the Wrong Type of Disintermediation—Counterfeiting

There is another type of disintermediation that is occurring, and it is one that must be stopped: counterfeiting. Some companies are using the same convergence of technology (cloud, mobility, SaaS, and data) that is positively shaping the future of business to help eliminate this threat.

Counterfeiting is a global problem and involves more than knock-off designer handbags. The proliferation of counterfeiting is impacting many industries, from printer and imaging supplies to pharmaceuticals, consumer electronics, and food and beverages. In some industries, such as pharmaceuticals, it can have deadly consequences. The International Policy Network reports that approximately 700,000 deaths per year are attributable to counterfeit malaria and tuberculosis drugs. Counterfeiting is taking its toll on businesses, too. It's estimated that $600 billion worth of world trade is attributed to counterfeit products each year.

Somewhere in the world, a consumer is about to buy an HP ink cartridge for an HP printer. The package looks legitimate and the seller says it's a genuine HP cartridge. But how can the consumer know it's real? Due to a sharp rise in counterfeiting, verifying a product's authenticity is harder than ever. In fact, the US Chamber of Commerce reports that 64% of counterfeit products are purchased in legitimate shops and retailers.

HP's Inkjet Printing and Solutions business, which sells millions of ink cartridges globally each year, has seen increased counterfeiting of its cartridges in recent years. And while HP has made progress curtailing counterfeiting, it did not really gain control of the problem until it launched a cloud-based anti-counterfeit solution. "We've seen efforts to counterfeit HP cartridges increase significantly in the last 10 years," says David Kellar, brand protection engineer for HP Inkjet and Printing Solutions. "And while we made progress against counterfeiters using solutions like hologram labels, it wasn't until we combined the cloud and mobile technology that we really got ahead of the issue."

In 2009, HP partnered with Brady Corporation, a leading provider of anti-counterfeit security labels, to create hologram labels for HP's ink cartridge packages. At the time, HP used a third-party platform to generate unique numeric codes for the hologram labels. However, HP realized that the numeric code platform wasn't powerful enough to generate codes at the speed and scale necessary for its cartridge business. Additionally, the platform didn't ensure the level of security HP wanted. HP also found that hologram labels, while adequate for some consumers, were too difficult to use for many. "If you know what to look for, there's great information in a hologram," Kellar says. "But for consumers who don't, they can be hard to read."

Realizing it needed a more powerful and secure numeric code generator, HP Inkjet and Printing Solutions (IPS) looked within and outside of HP. HP IPS found a solution through an affiliate business unit, HP Software Professional Services. Working in collaboration with HP Labs, HP Software Professional Services developed the underlying technology for what is now HP's Global Product Authentication Service (GPAS). What made HP's GPAS solution attractive is its numeric code encryption engine, which can quickly generate huge batches of numeric codes—a key capability for companies like HP that need to create millions of security labels each year. IPS went live with the HP GPAS in May 2012.

For Kellar, the GPAS solution is an indispensable tool for fighting counterfeiters. The GPAS Web Portal shows the products that are being counterfeited and the regions and cities where it's occurring. It also provides the business intelligence necessary to disrupt counterfeit activities. The GPAS Web Portal's real-time analytics include

- Geographic locations of valid security label authentications

- Geographic locations of invalid security label authentications

- Products that are most at risk to counterfeiting

- Trends showing geographic locations of potential counterfeiting

The GPAS Web Portal features heat maps that display where both valid and invalid security label authentications are taking place. A cluster of invalid labels indicates a hotspot of counterfeit activity. The heat maps allow HP Inkjet and Printing Solutions' brand manager to easily identify counterfeiting hotspots and act on them quickly.

HP's GPAS also enables consumers to easily authenticate genuine HP inkjet printer cartridges before making a purchase. Imagine a consumer wondering if the HP ink cartridge she is about to purchase is authentic. Using her smart phone and any standard Quick Response (QR) code reader, she would simply scan the security label on the HP ink cartridge box. If she doesn't own a smart phone, she would text the numbers on the security label. In either scenario, the consumer would immediately receive a message verifying if the security label's code is valid. If it isn't, the cartridge is probably a counterfeit and the consumer will receive information on how to report it. "Making the GPAS authentication technology so easy to use and accessible to consumers is a breakthrough," says Kellar.

Because the GPAS solution is hosted on HP's managed cloud environment, which scales rapidly, HP IPS launched the anti-counterfeit service quickly, without having to install any hardware or software. "Being a cloud solution, GPAS was easy to launch and caused no disruption to our business or supply chain," says Kellar. Thanks to this cloud architecture, GPAS is entirely accessible through the Web. Here's what makes HP GPAS work:

- **GPAS Secure Code Encryption Engine**—Generates unique and encrypted numeric codes for security labels

- **GPAS Secure Code Verification Database**—Receives consumers' QR code queries or SMS texts and verifies if a label has been validated

- **GPAS Web Portal**—Enables brand managers to access the anti-counterfeit solution; used for ordering codes for security labels, activating printers, and viewing real-time analytics

- **HP Converged Cloud Infrastructure**—Underpins HP's data center hosting service and provides mission-critical performance for HP GPAS

Running on HP's Enterprise Cloud Services cloud platform and managed by HP experts, GPAS features many benefits of cloud computing. It offers flexible pricing models, scale-up and scale-down capacity, massive compute power, and on-demand access. GPAS's Web self-service functionality makes it easy for brand and anti-counterfeit managers to use the service. They simply log in to the GPAS Web portal, and from there they can order secure codes or view a range of analytics reports.

While big brands have sought effective security labels for years, few solutions have generated unique security codes and labels fast enough. HP's GPAS addresses this. "Various security labeling solutions have emerged over the years, but none of them had the compute power to meet our manufacturing output, nor could they easily plug into our supply chain," says Kellar. "The cloud changes this."

In HP IPS's case, Brady Corporation orders and downloads unique numeric codes from the GPAS Web portal and then prints them on HP's ink cartridge security labels. Downloading the codes from the GPAS Web portal has accelerated Brady Corporation's label print preparation process. "The ability to download codes from the Web has greatly reduced the amount of time it takes us to prepare for a print production run," said Scott Kogler, senior product engineer for Brand Protection Solutions for Brady Corporation. "What used to require hours, we can now accomplish in minutes."

The improvement in speed is attributed to GPAS's Secure Code Encryption Engine. It can produce extremely large sets of unique numeric codes quickly, which is critical for companies that manufacture hundreds of millions of products. In the GPAS system, each security code has a unique, cryptographically secure number. The numbers can't be easily duplicated or changed in a predictable pattern, since that would allow counterfeiters to figure out the numeric codes and create fakes. The GPAS algorithm also enables the security code verification process. When a consumer scans or texts the code with their mobile phone, the algorithm queries the system's database to make sure the code hasn't already been validated. If it has, then the code isn't valid and the product is likely a counterfeit. All of this happens entirely in the cloud. With hundreds of millions of numbers in the GPAS Secure Code Verification database, speed is critical. The GPAS's cloud architecture allows consumers to verify a product's authenticity on the spot, whether they're shopping in a store in New York, Hong Kong, or Rio de Janeiro.

The HP GPAS is helping HP IPS protect its brand and market share. Every time a consumer identifies a counterfeit and buys a legitimate cartridge, HP protects revenue it would otherwise lose. Consumers get the genuine, high-quality HP cartridges they expect, and HP builds trust and loyalty with consumers by engaging them in the product authentication process.

3

Intellectual "Ditch Bag"

The underlying principles of strategy are enduring, regardless of technology or the pace of change.

—Michael Porter, author and professor, Harvard Business School

Early in my career I worked for Knight Ridder, a US media company specializing in newspaper and Internet publishing. Until it was acquired by the McClatchy Company in 2006, Knight Ridder was headquartered in San Jose, California (see Figure 3-1) and was America's second-largest newspaper publisher, with thirty-two daily newspapers.

The year was 1997, and I was the marketing manager for the *Miami Herald*, Knight Ridder's flagship newspaper property. At the time, newspapers survived or died based on print circulation, as measured and verified by the Audit Bureau of Circulation. Circulation drives readership. Readership drives advertising revenue.

Figure 3-1 Knight Ridder, once the second-largest newspaper conglomerate, was acquired in 2006. (Photo courtesy of John Pozniak.)

The late 1990s was a frustrating time for newspapers and for the *Miami Herald* in particular. Two squalls were approaching that would combine to create a storm that would forever affect the *Miami Herald*. First, there was a major demographic shift in the market area the paper served: Miami-Dade County's large Hispanic population had for decades been primarily of Cuban descent, but beginning in the 1980s, Miami began to become the "Capital of Latin America," and this trend exploded in the 1990s. Miami experienced an influx of Latin Americans from Columbia, Venezuela, Argentina, and even Mexico. By the 2000 census, over 57.3 percent of the population was Hispanic or Latino, and a remarkable 50.9 percent of the total population was foreign born.

These immigrants did not quickly assimilate into the American English-speaking culture, as immigrants traditionally had done throughout the history of the United States. Miami was the new "Capital of Latin America," and Spanish quickly became its predominant language. The *Miami Herald*, as an English-language ABC-audited publication, was at risk. This was the first squall.

The addition of the second squall created the perfect storm. In today's world, we take our access to much of our news and local information through the Internet as part of the fabric of our daily life. In the 1990s, it was just beginning. While America Online (AOL) was founded in 1985 as Quantum Computer Services, its remarkable growth really started in 1991, when Steve Case became CEO. Steve Case positioned AOL as the online service for people unfamiliar with computers. Beginning with online games, AOL added the now-famous "You've Got Mail," online chat, and a tremendous amount of content from repositories such as the Library of Congress and companies such as Pearson, Scholastic, and National Geographic. Soon, AOL was providing near-real-time news from media companies such as CNN and NPR. By 1997, about half of all homes with Internet access had it through AOL.

This inflection point had the potential to destroy the *Miami Herald*. The *Miami Herald* was an English-language newspaper in a Spanish-speaking city, and more and more consumers were getting their news from a new medium, the Internet.

It was during this time, at this inflection point, that an early mentor entered my career—Alberto Ibarguen. Alberto was born in Puerto Rico and raised in New Jersey. He graduated from Wesleyan University and went on to earn his law degree from the University of Pennsylvania Law School. Before entering law school, he served in the Peace Corps in Venezuela's Amazon Territory and in Colombia. In the corporate world, he spent time at the *Hartford Courant* and eleven years at *Newsday* in New York, and eventually he became publisher of the Miami Herald Publishing Company. He had the great pleasure of taking that position at the height of the storm hitting the *Miami Herald*.

Alberto knew that the *Herald* had to do things differently if it was going to survive. It had a Spanish-language supplement, *El Herald*, but *El Herald* was not an independent, ABC-audited newspaper. It had a fledgling English-language website with very few resources, and circulation and advertising revenue were starting to experience serious downward pressures.

Alberto asked me to join a team that would prepare and implement a strategic plan to address these inflection points. I became the program lead of that group with our Hispanic Marketing Manager Miguel Pereira as a key advisor. Miguel continues to have a very successful career now as founder and CEO of SocialNoise, a noteworthy digital creative agency in Spain and Mexico. Alberto reminded us about our core competency—creating, gathering, and disseminating content of interest to the community. He also reminded us that while content is the core, the language and method of receiving that content are ultimately up to the consumer. The *Miami Herald* needed to have an operating environment that was capable of continual transformation. At the core, it had to have robust content creation and aggregation. But the operating model had to be flexible in order to distribute that content in Spanish or English as well as in print or digitally. If we could do this, we would have competitive advantage in the marketplace.

During that period, the working group segmented the marketplace by language preference into what we called Spanish influence groups, and we provided the resources and mechanisms to go to market in both print and on the Internet. *El Nuevo Herald* (see Figure 3-2) launched as an independent, ABC-audited, Spanish-language newspaper in 1998. Elnuevoherald.com was launched simultaneously, as were other digital and print specialty publications, such as *Viernes*. Within a year, *El Nuevo Herald* became the largest Spanish-language newspaper in the United States. The combined audited circulation of the English- and Spanish-language products allowed the *Miami Herald* to enjoy the largest circulation and readership growth in 1998 of any newspaper in the United States. And seventeen years later, both flagship properties are thriving in print and online.

Figure 3-2 *El Nuevo Herald* launched in 1998 and was soon the largest Spanish-language newspaper in the United States.

My experience at the *Miami Herald* was one of many that helped me understand the three foundational principles that I want my clients to understand when I consult with them:

• Core competency

• Competitive advantage

• Continual transformation environment

These are the contents of my intellectual "ditch bag," and they are just as important to me, and as carefully assembled, as the ditch bag that helped my family survive Tropical Storm Alex.

Most businesspeople have some familiarity with at least the first two of these business concepts, but I want to make sure that we all share an understanding of what they mean and what they imply about how business leaders should be thinking about IT, so I'll delve a little deeper into each concept.

Core Competency

Dr. Paul Shoemaker first introduced me to the concept of a company's core competency while I was working for Knight Ridder. Paul is an expert in the field of strategic management. He is currently the research director at the Mack Institute for Innovation Management at the Wharton School of the University of Pennsylvania, where he also teaches decision making and strategy. In the late 1990s, I had the pleasure of working with Paul and his firm, Decision Strategies International, in a strategic planning engagement. Dr. Shoemaker uses a scenario-planning approach to strategic planning, and understanding a company's core competency in the context of scenario planning is critical.

C. K. Prahalad and Gary Hamel introduced the idea of "core competencies" nearly twenty-five years ago in a Harvard Business Review article titled "The Core Competence of the Corporation." Prahalad was a professor of Corporate Strategy at the Stephen M. Ross School of Business at the University of Michigan. Until his death in 2013, he was one of the world's most prominent business thinkers. Gary Hamel is a professor at the London Business School and was recently ranked by the *Wall Street Journal* as the world's most influential business thinker. Together, Prahalad and Hamel expanded on their *HBR* article in a book called *Competing for the Future* (see Figure 3-3).

Figure 3-3 The concept of core competency was first introduced by Prahalad and Hamel more than 25 years ago. (Cover design by Mike Fender. Copyright © 1994 by Harvard Business Publishing; all rights reserved.)

According to Prahalad and Hamel, a core competency is "a harmonized combination of multiple resources and skills that distinguish a firm in the marketplace." Core competencies fulfill three criteria:

- They can create access to a wide variety of markets.
- They make a significant contribution to a company's customers.
- They are difficult for competitors to imitate.

For example, a company whose core competencies include precision mechanics, fine optics, and micro-electronics will be well suited to building cameras, which may result in that company becoming known primarily as a camera maker. But these core competencies may also be useful to the company in making other products that require this particular know-how, such as optical sensors. Honda's core competency is the design and manufacture of engines and drivetrains. This core competency supports product lines in automotive, motorcycles, boating, lawn mowers, and even generators. With that in mind, you would not see Honda extend its product line into televisions, which is unrelated to its core competency.

In their *HBR* article, Prahalad and Hamel show that core competencies help companies develop core products, and these core products in turn lead to the development of a much more diverse set of products for customers. Core competencies are defined and refined through a process of continual improvements over time rather than through a single large change. Competence building is an outcome of strategic architecture, which must be enforced by top management in order to exploit its full capacity.

A focus on core competencies is even more important during inflection points if companies can see the change coming. In *Competing for the Future*, Hamel and Prahalad demonstrate how executives can acquire the foresight necessary to adapt to changes in their industries and how they can learn to control resources in ways that will enable the companies they work for to achieve their goals despite any constraints.

In today's ever-changing and disruptive environments, a company must regain focus on its core competency. In fact, it must have a fanatical focus on its core competency and free up management bandwidth and capital for that focus.

Competitive Advantage

Harvard Business School professor Michael Porter is an authority on competitive strategy and the author of *Competitive Advantage*. Porter argues that an organization gains competitive advantage when it develops attributes that enable it to outperform its competitors. These attributes can take a variety of forms:

- Access to natural resources, such as high-grade ores or inexpensive power
- Access to skilled employees

- New technologies (such as robotics and information technology), which can provide an advantage as a part of the product itself, in the manufacture of a product, or in the selling of a product

Porter believes that the primary concern of strategic management should be building and maintaining competitive advantage. This means staying ahead of present or potential future competition in order to become and stay a market leader.

Porter advocates these four major strategies for building competitive advantage:

- **Cost leadership strategy**—The object of cost leadership as a strategy is to offer products or services at the lowest cost in the industry. Walmart, for example, succeeds by offering low prices on items whose prices matter to its customers and selling other merchandise at less significant discounts.

- **Differentiation strategy**—Differentiation strategy aims to provide products, services, or features to consumers that competitors do not offer. Dell, for example, offered mass customizations of computers before its competitors did.

- **Innovation strategy**—The goal of innovation strategy is to get ahead of other market players by introducing completely new or markedly better products or services. Apple exemplifies this strategy through its introduction of iPod personal music players, the iPhone, and the iPad tablets.

- **Operational effectiveness strategy**—The goal of an operational effectiveness strategy is to be better at internal business activities than one's competitors, thereby making one's own company easier to do business with than other market choices.

Porter's "Five Forces Analysis" is a framework that a company can use to analyze the level of competition within an industry and then develop an appropriate business strategy. These five forces determine the competitive intensity within the marketplace and, therefore, the attractiveness of a market (i.e., industry profitability).

A change in any of these forces requires a business to reassess the marketplace. In today's disruptive marketplace, companies must be able to reassess and react almost instantaneously. This might involve exiting markets, entering markets, acquiring, divesting, changing channels of distribution, creating a new distribution channel, etc.

These are Porter's five forces:

- **Threat of new entrants**—Profitable markets will always attract new entrants, which will eventually decrease profitability throughout the industry. Unless new firms can be prevented from entering the market, the industry's profit rate will begin to approach zero. Amazon not only entered the book distribution market but entered the publishing sector through facilitating the creation and distribution of self-published books, dramatically reducing the overall sector's margins.

- **Threat of substitute products or services**—The existence of products outside common product boundaries increases the likelihood that customers will switch to alternatives. For example, Coca-Cola has long considered Pepsi to be its competitor because it sells a similar product. But a potential consumer might also consider bottled water as a substitute for Coke, even though the product itself is dissimilar. Increased marketing for bottled water might decrease the market share for both Coke and Pepsi, whereas increased Coca-Cola advertising would likely "grow the pie" for Coke and Pepsi alike—and also increase consumption of all soft drinks. Today, Uber has totally disrupted the taxicab industry, serving as an example of what the threat of a substitute product or service can have in the marketplace.

- **Bargaining power of customers**—This is the ability of customers to put the firm under pressure, which affects the customer's sensitivity to price changes. Buyer power is high if a buyer has many alternatives; buyer power is low if he or she has to act independently. Firms can reduce buyer power by taking actions such as implementing loyalty programs. The disintermediation of retailers in favor of online marketplaces such as Amazon, eBay, Etsy, and Alibaba has aggregated massive numbers of consumers placing tremendous downward price pressure on suppliers.

- **Bargaining power of suppliers**—Suppliers of raw materials, components, labor, and services (such as expertise) can leverage power over a firm when few substitutes are available. If you make biscuits, and there is only one seller of flour, you have no choice but to buy flour from that supplier. This puts the supplier in a position of power; it may refuse to work with your firm if it dislikes doing business with you, or it may charge excessively high prices.

- **Intensity of competitive rivalry**—The four forces cited above all exert pressure on the fifth force: the intensity of the competition. Some industries may have only one or two forces at work, and in a limited way, so the intensity of industry rivalry is minimal. A company should be able to ride this scenario to growth and profit. Other industries may have all five forces exerting tremendous pressure. This industry may be low growth, low margin, and commoditized. For most industries, the intensity of competitive rivalry is a major determinant of the growth potential of a company.

Core Competency and Competitive Advantage Working Together

Core competency and competitive advantage are of absolute necessity for today's business success. The business environment is changing. We are in a disruptive time, and the *speed* of change is increasing. To survive, companies must instill a fanatical focus on their core competency; a company must refocus its management bandwidth and assets directly on its core competency. In addition, companies must continually look for competitive advantage. This is not a once-every-few-years strategic planning process. Companies must continually, each and every day, use the principles of Porter's Five Forces Analysis to constantly reassess where they stand in terms of competitive advantage.

So, once a company has a fanatical focus on its core competency and is constantly assessing its competitive advantage, how does it react to approaching squalls and storms?

Continual Transformation Environment

I began to think about the concept of continual transformation environment (CTE) as a business operating principle in the mid-2000s, while serving as vice president at Inforte Corporation. Inforte, started by Phil Bligh, was one of the first customer relationship management consultancies. Phil also co-authored *CRM Unplugged* (see Figure 3-4). Gartner said of Inforte, "So, when you research a consulting organization that does stand out—based on its focus, thought leadership, and capabilities—it is worth noting. Inforte clearly stands out in the crowded world of Customer Relationship Management (CRM) consultancies." Gartner placed Inforte in the top "Visionary" spot in its CRM magic quadrant, where it beat out the likes of Accenture and IBM. Phil took this company from an idea to a very successful IPO through his vision and by surrounding himself with strategic thinkers. He had the foresight to bring together a dynamic board of directors that included Michael Porter, Philip Kotler, and Ray Kurzweil, among others, to mentor the company's leadership.

Figure 3-4 Inforte's success was based on a singular focus on CRM.

At Inforte, I was introduced to Ray Kurzweil. Kurzweil is an American author, computer scientist, inventor, and futurist. A graduate of MIT, he has written books on health, artificial intelligence (AI), transhumanism, technological singularity, and futurism. Among numerous other innovations, Kurzweil invented the first CCD flatbed scanner, and President Clinton presented him with the 1999 National Medal of Technology and Innovation, the U.S. government's highest technology honor.

The *Wall Street Journal* has described Kurzweil as a "restless genius," and *Forbes* has called him "the ultimate thinking machine." PBS once included him on a list of sixteen "revolutionaries who made America," and *Inc.* magazine ranked him eighth on its list of the "26 most fascinating entrepreneurs" in the United States, calling him "Edison's rightful heir."

In his 2001 essay "The Law of Accelerating Returns," Kurzweil talks about technology-driven change. Many people are concerned about the continued progression of technology and the impact it has on business. Kurzweil says that it is not just technology that is progressing; the rate of change itself is accelerating exponentially:

> Our forebears expected the future to be pretty much like their present, which had been pretty much like their past. Although exponential trends did exist a thousand years ago, they were at that very early stage where an exponential trend is so flat that it looks like no trend at all. So their lack of expectations was largely fulfilled. Today, in accordance with the common wisdom, everyone expects continuous technological progress and the social repercussions that follow. But the future will be far more surprising than most observers realize: few have truly internalized the implications of the fact that the rate of change itself is accelerating.

Today's business environment is arguably the most dynamic in history. In the past, industries might have gone decades or even centuries without much change to their basic marketplaces. Today, however, the value chain and go-to-market models in many industry sectors are approaching real-time disruption. Companies and entire industries are disappearing within months due to disintermediation and the impact of today's inflection point. New companies, industries and sectors are being created overnight, and entire segments of the value and supply chains are being removed or changed. Every aspect of a company's product or service life cycle can now dramatically change in a business instant.

Kurzweil's teachings, coupled with my own prior experience, have been codified into the CTE operating model. An operating model takes a complex system like an organization and shows how it works by breaking it down into components. It can help the various participants in the organization to understand the whole, and it can help those who are making changes to ensure that the whole will still work after those changes have been made. It can help those who are transforming an operation coordinate all the changes that need to be made. In the CTE operating model, the company has very little reliance on anything "fixed." Operating flexibility is the new mantra. Change and innovation are embraced throughout the organization. Fixed assets are shed in favor of consumption-based enablers. Static internal business functions are shed in favor of business-outcomes-based service providers.

In a CTE environment, we have to rethink even the way the company is defined. A "company-owned" organization is composed of what is needed to nourish the company's core competencies. All other functions are provided by an ecosystem of trusted partners. This narrowed-down focus on a company's core competency allows the company to have a fanatical focus on flexibility, change, transformation, and innovation powered by its core competency, unimpeded by fixed assets and processes that would forever lock the company into a fixed, inflexible path.

There are five pillars of the CTE operating model:

1. "Company-owned" business functions must be directly tied to the company's core competency.
2. Non-core competency functions are "divested" from the company and provided by an ecosystem of trusted partners.
3. An ecosystem of providers provides services in a utility, consumption-based model.
4. Return on invested capital (ROIC) and total shareholder return (TSR) replace earnings before interest taxes depreciation and amortization (EBITDA) as key metrics.
5. The operational IT business unit provides the foundation of the CTE operating model and must be a service broker for the ecosystem of providers.

Companies that instill the CTE operating model are nimble, flexible, and ever changing. They turn on a dime, in a millisecond.

The Three Foundation Principles Working Together

The intellectual "ditch bag" I bring with me to every client includes these three foundation principles—core competency, competitive advantage, and continual transformation environment—and the interactions among them. There will be storms and inflection points for every industry, sector, and business. And as modernity advances, the waves from these storms are going to hit harder and more frequently.

Whether a company survives these inflection points will be determined by its focus and ability to continually transform. A company that has a fanatical focus on its core competency and is not burdened by the fixed assets, structures, and processes of the old-school operating models will thrive. A company with a focus on core competency enhanced by a continual transformation environment operating model can change, react, grow, and thrive in the harshest of disruptive environments. Such companies can react swiftly to the forces around them and ensure their competitive advantage.

Tribune Company—A Tale of Survival

I took my intellectual ditch bag with me a few years ago when I went to see Sam Zell's management, right after he purchased the Tribune Company. The experience provides a powerful lesson in dealing with inflection points.

The *Chicago Tribune* is one of the nation's leading newspapers. Founded in 1847, it once proudly boasted on its front page that it was "The World's Greatest Newspaper." In the course of its history, it is has featured such outstanding writers as Ring Lardner, movie critic Gene Siskel, and columnists Clarence Page and Mike Royko. It has won twenty-five Pulitzer Prizes for journalistic excellence, including five in the first years of the twenty-first century. The *Tribune* gained historical infamy in 1948 when, before all votes were counted, it declared on its front page "Dewey Defeats Truman."

The next day, the new president-elect Harry Truman immortalized the error by holding up the paper for a photo for posterity.

Over time, the *Tribune* morphed into a major media player called the Tribune Company, which came to own thirty-nine local television stations, two superstations, and nine major newspapers, including the *Los Angeles Times*. It also became the owner of the Chicago Cubs, one of the city's two baseball teams.

In December 2007, Chicago billionaire Sam Zell bought the Tribune Company through a leveraged buyout for $8.2 billion. He became the company's new chair and took it private.

It was a remarkable year for Sam. He sold Equity Office Properties Trust, an office owner, to the Blackstone Group for $39 billion while still heading up Equity Residential, the largest publically traded apartment landlord.

In early 2008, I held discussions with Sam's management team in an attempt to help the company. I had worked for a number of years on the business side of the Knight Ridder newspaper chain, and we had quite a few joint partnerships with the Tribune Company. I had personal experience with what it took for newspapers to compete in the twenty-first century, in the face of the Internet and rapidly declining circulation and advertising revenues. About a year before I met with Sam's team, I had outlined my approach in *Editor & Publisher*, the trade journal for the newspaper industry (see Figure 3-5). There I laid out a wide-ranging plan that all newspapers had to consider.

EDITOR&PUBLISHER

REPRINTED FROM JULY 2006

Shoptalk

TIME FOR NEW MODEL

Newspapers must rethink their approach in seven key areas

FOR YEARS, MANY HAVE FORECAST THE DEATH OF THE traditional newspaper. Certainly the business model employed by current newspaper chains is not sustainable in the long term. However, a rapid deployment of a new business model would lead to long-term growth. At its foundation, the newspaper company of the future is a content company. Its mission of gathering and disseminating information is sacrosanct. Whether that information is disseminated via print, Web, or wireless is of no consequence.

To restore long-term sustainable growth, today's newspaper chains must quickly adopt the following model.

1. EDITORIAL. Protect the local editorial function. This is the core asset of the newspaper. Provide the tools, budget, and personnel to gather information in multiple formats. The day has arrived where a publishing company does not necessarily need to own a television license to provide broadcast content. Utilizing the core aspects of digital asset management, centralize the technology platform used by the editorial function through one enterprise platform, Web-enabled and hosted by a third-party provider.

2. ACCOUNTING. Centralize all accounting functions. Many have already been centralized; now, the last remaining functions — advertising billing and subscription billing — must follow suit. The technology platform for all accounting functions should be a central, Web-enabled platform most likely hosted by a third party.

3. CIRCULATION. Centralize circulation customer service and outsource it to a third party. Also, centralize the home-subscriber marketing function and support it with a customer-information marketing technology platform hosted by a third party. Once centralized, most of the process can be outsourced to a direct marketing agency with experience in acquisition and retention marketing.

4. ADVERTISING. Newspapers must base their advertising sales process on overall reach, not mere print circulation. Reach is a combination of the print publication, Web sites, podcasts, wireless, and the like. Advertising sales representatives must sell reach. Thus, ROP must be redefined as Run of Product, not Run of Press.

The Audit Bureau of Circulation (ABC) must follow suit and change its reporting to overall reach, not just print circ. If the ABC is unwilling to change with the times, then newspapers should abandon ABC reporting altogether. As long as it is replaced by a reliable mechanism to measure reach, there are many of us who believe that abandoning ABC reporting would not have serious negative consequences in the advertising community. By the way, I am not suggesting doing this in a few years, but by the end of *this* year.

Advertising sales must primarily remain a local function, with a strong national sales force representing the entire chain. National sales should be supported by a sales force automation platform most likely provided through an application service provider. Private-party classified advertising should be centralized and probably outsourced — most likely to the same third-party provider used for circulation customer service. Internet advertising sales should not be sold by a separate sales force.

However, the newspaper chains need to open themselves up to the advertising sales and delivery mechanisms of some of the larger Internet players like Google and Yahoo. Their advertising programs are generating large revenue gains from which newspapers' well-trafficked sites would greatly benefit.

5. PRODUCTION. As newspaper chains become fully paginated, outsourcing production becomes less of an issue. Local advertisers still have a demand for advertising production, whether in print or on the Web. Several newspapers have shown successfully that this business process can and should be outsourced to a third party.

6. PRINTING. Outsource the printing business function. Yes, I am suggesting that newspapers divest their printing facilities. Firms that specialize in printing are better suited to optimize other potential revenue from these fixed assets while, on a contract basis, providing the day-to-day printing needed for the daily newspaper. Newspapers would be surprised at the interest level shown in the auction process.

7. DISTRIBUTION. Outsource the distribution business function. Yes, I am suggesting that newspapers sell off their distribution facilities as well. As with printing, firms that specialize in distribution are better suited to optimize ROI on these assets. Meanwhile, these firms can provide a newspaper's print distribution on a contract basis.

Will today's newspaper chains take a short-term hit from these steps? Most likely, yes. However, once business processes are consolidated at the enterprise level — or outsourced, if they are not core competencies — the publishing firm will be a nimble player in content creation, aggregation, and distribution regardless of the medium.

Scott Stawski leads the marketing solutions practice at Knightsbridge Solutions, a consulting firm in Chicago, Ill.

BY SCOTT STAWSKI

Printed in USA. Vol. 139, No. 7, EDITOR & PUBLISHER (ISSN: 0013-094X, USPS: 168-320) is published 12 times a year. Regular issues are published monthly by VNU Business Publications USA, 770 Broadway, N.Y., NY 10003. Sales (Fax) 646-654-5360; Editorial (646) 654-5263. Periodicals postage paid at New York, NY, and additional mailing offices. Postmaster: Please send address changes to: EDITOR & PUBLISHER, THE FOURTH ESTATE, P.O. Box 16016, N. Hollywood, CA 91615-9440. Copyright 2006, VNU Business Media Inc. No part of this publication may be reproduced, stored in any retrieval system, or transmitted, in any form or by any means, electronic, mechanical, photocopying or otherwise, without the prior written permission of the publisher. For reprints, please call Wright's Reprints (877) 652-5295. Annual subscription $99 in the U.S. and possessions and in Canada. Foreign surface $140 and foreign air $320. Canadian Publication Mail Agreement No. 40031736. Return Undeliverable Canadian Addresses to: Deutsche Post Global Mail 4960-2, Walker Road, Windsor, ON N9A 6J3. No claim for back issues honored after one year. From time to time, E&P may allow reputable companies to send information that may be of interest by mail or e-mail. If you do not want to receive this information, please advise Subscriber Service by either telephone or e-mail (including E&P in your subject heading). Subscriber Service (800) 562-2706. Customer Service E-mail: editorandpublisher@espcomp.com

Figure 3-5 Stawski's article on a drastic transformation of the newspaper operating model created a lot of controversy when it was first published. However, many of the recommendations have now been implemented by newspapers.

I began the article talking about getting newspapers to focus on their core competency, which to my mind was content: the aggregation and dissemination of information, regardless of the delivery medium—print, broadcast, or digital. Above all, I supported protecting the editorial function of a newspaper, but I argued that the storage of this content needed to be centralized, fully digitized, and indexed for repurposing. Primarily, I proposed that newspaper and multi-media chains must consolidate most of their non-editorial functions into shared service environments and then outsource most of those functions.

I similarly proposed that all accounting for advertising and subscription billing needed to be centralized and handled by a third party.

I went through other vital elements of change for newspapers. Finance, accounting, and billing needed to be centralized, as did circulation and customer service, and they needed to be handed over to a third party. I noted that the same centralization and outsourcing should occur in the subscriber marketing function, supported by a customer information marketing technology platform—again hosted by a third party. Once centralized, I said, these business functions could be outsourced to a direct marketing agency with experience in acquisition and retention marketing.

I proposed a fundamentally new way to think about advertising. I believed it should be based on overall reach, not just print circulation. *Reach* should be defined as print plus websites plus podcasts plus mobile. Advertising representatives should sell reach. The long-held newspaper advertising idea of "ROP" needed to be redefined as "run of product," not "run of press."

Still, advertising needed to remain a local function with strong national representation. Sales should be supported by a sales force automation platform. This would be provided through an application service provider. Private-party classified advertising should be centralized and outsourced, most likely to the same third-party provider used for circulation and customer service. Further, newspaper chains needed to open themselves up to the advertising sales and digital advertising delivery mechanisms of large Internet companies like Google. As for advertising production for local advertisers, this still seemed to be a service that newspapers could provide—but it could be outsourced also.

In the article, I argued that the printing function of newspapers should be outsourced. No element of change was so difficult for newspaper people to accept. The presses had always represented the power of the papers, a belief that is highlighted in great movies from *The Front Page* to *Citizen Kane* to *All the President's Men*. But in the twenty-first century, there are firms that specialize in printing, and these companies are better suited to optimize newspaper presses for other potential revenues if they engage these specialists on a contract basis. A highly priced fixed asset should not sit idle for sixteen hours a day.

In addition, I pointed out, digital personalized printing—both high speed and high volume—was on the horizon. Newspapers could quickly adopt personalized a la carte newspaper printing and delivery.

My final recommendation also struck at the romance of the press: distribution. The newspaper flung on the porch at six o'clock in the morning, or hawked on city sidewalks by paperboys shouting headlines, was the essence of the constant presence of a great paper like the *Chicago Tribune*. Each newspaper delivery service is essentially a private, single-purpose postal service. It is horribly inefficient, and for newspapers to survive, I argued, it had to end. Delivery needed to be outsourced, and the distribution facilities needed to be sold off.

The reception to the article was highly favorable. It led to a keynote address at a Newspaper Association of America conference, and it provided the outline of what I was going to suggest to Sam and his buyout team when we met.

Sam is an impressive man—bald, goateed, blunt, and prone to wearing blue jeans to work. I told Sam's team that the paper would not be able to make its debt payments with its fixed infrastructure and costs distracting from its core competency, and I told him about the necessary changes newspapers had to make in the new digital world. I predicted a rapid decline of classified and display advertising and subscription revenue. I recommended that the *Trib* sell off its printing presses, as I had suggested in the article.

Sam's team countered that no company would ever consider buying a newspaper's printing operations. Today, as one example, Transcontinental now prints more than 150 newspapers, including the Toronto Globe. I argued for entering into distribution agreements with UPS, FedEx, or the US Postal Service. Sam's team said USPS would never negotiate delivery with a private company, and trying to chase such an agreement would be time wasted. Just a few years later, however, Amazon reached an agreement with USPS for Sunday delivery, among other things.

As for IT, I followed the same logic: outsource anything that wasn't directly part of the core competency and move it to an ecosystem of partners in a consumption-based environment. I actually suggested that the *Trib* deliberately take down its circulation by switching readers from print to digital: I suggested that the *Tribune* offer a free or discounted laptop or Internet access to subscribers who were willing to convert. All these recommendations together could have saved the *Tribune* $500 million annually.

How did Sam's team react to my extensive suggestions? Basically, they said, "Don't call us, we'll call you." And, we never heard from Sam's team again. They believed they had time for incremental change against the inflection point of that time—readers and advertisers leaving the print product for a digital alternative. They didn't buy into the idea that massive change was necessary.

By the end of 2008, the Tribune Company had filed for bankruptcy protection, following a $124 million third-quarter loss on the newspaper. Zell cited a debt of $13 billion and assets of $7.6 billion as reasons for this filing. I guess that bankruptcy and losing ownership of the *Tribune* were probably good reasons I never heard back from Sam's team.

But Sam is not alone. Since 2007, more than one hundred fifty metropolitan newspapers have gone out of business because they have not gotten in front of the inflection point and the ensuing business disruption.

The Tribune Media has since emerged from bankruptcy and is now partially owned by private equity firms, including Oaktree Capital.

Tribune Publishing—which includes the *Chicago Tribune* and the *Los Angeles Times*, among other newspapers—was spun off as a separate, NYSE publicly traded company in August 2014. From my perspective, their new management team is world-class, and they are much more open to meaningful transformation.

4

Information Technology as a Utility

We are stuck with technology when what we really want is just stuff that works.

—Douglas Adams, author, *The Hitchhiker's Guide to the Galaxy*

In sailing, each member of my family definitely has his or her own particular areas of responsibility—or core competencies. Knowing our roles and sticking to our core competencies adds enjoyment to our sailing experience and makes it safer.

As the captain, I have ultimate responsibility for our fifty-foot sailboat and all onboard. I perform safety checks, and I am the skipper. I choose the course, do the primary sailing, and take personal accountability for everything that happens during our trip. My wife, Hope, is our cruise director and executive chef, and she and my son, Henry, assist with the actual sailing. They can jibe and tack with the best of them; they can handle all the sheets (the actual sails—main, head, storm, and jib), and they are both very good at following directions. Our boat has a nine-foot semi-rigid inflatable boat called a *dinghy*—it's a small boat with a hard bottom, inflatable sides, and an outboard engine. This is what we use to get back and forth whenever we drop anchor and leave the boat to go exploring and diving. Henry is the dinghy captain.

Over the years, each of us has developed a core competency related to the experience of sailing. My core competencies are sailing the boat and safety. Henry's is the dinghy. Hope is the chef, organizer, and social director. I don't want to downplay her role in actual sailing, but she's unparalleled at stocking the boat and making the most of a limited amount of storage. She secures all the supplies and uses them to make the most fantastic gourmet meals in the world. No dining experience at a restaurant can compare with the meals she makes for us. She sets our itinerary, plans our activities, and makes all arrangements on land. She is the model of organization. In fact, maybe she is really in charge, and I just think I am the captain?

So now let me tell you a story about what happens when you step outside your core competency.

One of our many sailing expeditions took us off the coast of Florida, to Key West and Bimini, and as far north as Fort Lauderdale. It was an eventful trip, on which we gave what's called a "sailor's funeral" to our Uncle Roger.

We met up with other parts of the family—landlubbers who flew down and stayed in a rented house, with plans to rent a powerboat to meet us out at sea for Uncle Roger's sailor's funeral. We three Stawskis were on a sailing vacation. We were there to celebrate Roger's life and participate in his sailor's funeral, but the funeral was only one part of our trip.

We were anchored about a mile off the coast of Florida. I was napping, and my wife and son had decided to take the dinghy out to visit the rest of the family on shore. They have a small dock, and the water is so shallow there that we needed to anchor our boat about a mile out. My son's core competency is dinghy captaining (see Figure 4-1), so we were very confident. He has his dinghy ditch bag and his emergency equipment, so we agreed that I'd stay on the sailboat and that Henry would take Hope in to shore for a visit.

Figure 4-1 Henry's core competency as the dinghy captain.

A few hours later, the sun had gone down, and I got a call from Henry on our marine VHF, informing me that he'd be staying overnight at the house with his cousins and that Hope had decided to pilot the dinghy the mile back to the boat. I immediately said no. We'd never taught Hope how to use the dinghy on the open ocean; it's not her core competency, and there is a big gap between her current proficiency with the dingy and the manner in which she was planning to operate it—that gap being what she needs to learn to be truly safe in operating a dinghy for a trip of this length.

Then my son said, "Oh, well...she already left."

Panic set in. Thirty minutes passed, then forty-five minutes, then an hour. She should have been able to reach the boat in about ten or fifteen minutes with the dinghy. I had the binoculars out and was hailing her on the VHF radio, and my anxiety was rising by the minute.

Finally I heard a crackling on the VHF radio. She had a hand-held radio with her, and I could hear the panic in her voice. She was somewhere between the boat and the land, but she was having a very difficult time controlling the dinghy. You have to understand: in most sailboat tenders or dinghies, there is no steering wheel. You use the position of the engine as the rudder to steer. And, unless you're trained on it, a dinghy is much more difficult to point in the proper direction than it appears to be. You have to deal with the wind, the tides, and a very strong Gulf Stream; and now the sun had set, and it was dark. She was zigzagging, and the more she thought she was aiming toward the boat, the farther away from it she got. There was a good chance she was going to run out of gas and float into the wide Atlantic.

I could not see her. At times she saw the boat, and at times she didn't. She was flying blind, and our ability to locate her was based largely on the strength of her radio signal.

In a panic, she suggested that maybe she should just jump off and swim for the boat the next time she saw it in the distance. She's an excellent swimmer, but that was a horrible idea. Again, if sailing isn't your core competency, you don't understand the strength of the tides and the Gulf Stream. So I calmed her down and explained that NO, she was to stay on the dinghy—*no matter what.*

After about two hours of this back-and-forth, she finally made it to within twenty or thirty feet of the boat. She was exhausted and had a hard time bringing the dinghy in. It was about midnight, the waves were stronger, and it was pitch dark.

Finally she got to a place where I could throw her a rope and bring her onboard. What a wave of relief. That was the most frightened I have ever been when sailing—even more frightened than during the tropical storm we went through that later turned into Hurricane Alex—because I had no control over the situation, and she was performing a role that she was not trained for—a role that was not her core competency.

We wonder all the time why companies try to do things outside their core competencies. Is it overconfidence? Is it failure to understand that a fanatical focus on your core competency is essential for success? In today's dynamic business environment, companies must concentrate on their core competencies and let trusted firms in the ecosystem around them concentrate on the activities outside those core competencies. This is how you build the continual transformation environment operating model that will give you competitive advantage.

My family's core competencies allow us to weather any storm and always have an enjoyable experience. That situation with Hope off the coast of Florida certainly taught us that no one should ever step outside of his or her core competency—at least on our boat!

If core competencies are such an important concept, and if influential business consultants have been talking about them since the idea was introduced by Prahalad and Hamel a quarter century ago, why do so many companies struggle to understand it? Why do so many businesses fail to focus on their own core competencies?

Part of the answer lies in the fact that it's hard for businesses to think about the future, and it's easy for them to steer slightly off course. Companies in today's marketplace face a wide variety of concerns and never-ending fire drills that keep them so occupied with solving whatever problem is right in front of them that they often are unable to see any farther out. To make matters worse, their IT operations lock them into an inflexible operating model instead of the utility model that the convergence of today's technology provides. Therefore, they don't have the continual transformation environment necessary for competitive advantage.

This is a reason businesses hire consultants: consultants bring a fresh perspective and see the organization from the outside, without getting bogged down by the company's day-to-day problem solving. It's a consultant's job to see things about the company that people inside it can't see for themselves.

In the consulting world, we talk about "CMO"—the current mode of operation—and about "FMO"—the future mode of operation. We analyze the gaps between current mode and future mode, and we ask, "How can we become fanatically focused on our core competency? What does the future mode of operation look like? And what needs to happen, for example, to IT infrastructure, IT software, data, and mobility for the company to move to a continual transformation environment operating model?"

When advising companies, part of my job is helping top management look into the future—in particular, the future of optimal business enablers. In the future, I tell them, they will be able to spend as much as 40 percent less on IT, and the money they do spend will be on a pure consumption, pay for usage model. In the future, IT will be an operating expense requiring no capital expense. IT departments will not run data centers, buy software, or manage applications. Instead, the IT department of the future will be a service broker for an ecosystem of trusted providers of technology enablers to their business users. Business IT will be consumerized with self-service access to technology enablers and data necessary for the user's business function. This nimble, flexible IT environment is at the heart of the continual transformation environment operating model.

In this future, companies will consume IT the way that people currently consume electricity: when we need light, we flip a switch, and at the end of the month, we pay a bill for the services we use. The average consumer doesn't buy power generators and electrical lines and infrastructure but just partners with a company that provides electricity. Similarly, IT departments will soon stop worrying about what servers the company should buy or whether to buy Oracle Database 12c or Microsoft SQL Server 2014 for their database needs. These worries will be obsolete because IT departments will have partners within their ecosystems to deliver the functional value of these enablers directly to business users, eliminating the need for the company to invest in so much capital infrastructure and fixed IT assets and leaving the business and its users free to concentrate on their core competencies.

In fact, in the future, corporate IT will be much less visible, and that is a good thing! The less visible corporate IT is to the business user, the more value those business users are getting from their technology enablers, and the more management bandwidth can be spent on the company's core competency. The management bandwidth we spend so much time on today—the technology behind the enablers—will and must become a thing of the past. Instead, the chief information officer will be tasked with ensuring that the company's business users and leadership have access to whatever relevant enabler and data they need in a true utility fashion.

Right now, company management teams spend far too much time dealing with IT. From what I've seen, it's considered business as usual for company leadership and senior management to burn 10 to 15 percent of their time on IT discussions or issues. They might be involved in gathering requirements for a new financial system. They might have to review a status report from IT on issues related to the company's supply-chain management system. They will attend meetings about replacing aging IT infrastructure. They do all these things instead of doing what they were hired to do: use their core competencies to create competitive advantage.

In the future, many of these meetings and reports will be eliminated, freeing business users and management to do their jobs. One company that is rapidly moving to this future is Deutsche Bank. In February 2015 Deutsche Bank and Hewlett Packard Enterprise announced a ten-year agreement that will further modernize the bank's global information technology environment and will aim to significantly reduce related IT infrastructure costs.

Under the terms of the agreement, which mainly covers wholesale banking IT infrastructure, HP will provide dedicated data center services on demand, including storage, platform, and hosting. As part of a wider IT transformation program, Deutsche Bank will upgrade and reduce the number of its IT applications, move them on to the HP platform, and enhance its own processes for providing technology support to its operations.

Henry Ritchotte, Chief Operating Officer of Deutsche Bank, said, "This agreement enables Deutsche Bank to secure standardized, world-class IT infrastructure while lowering costs. Having a more modern and agile technology platform will further improve the bank's ability to launch new products and services and lay the foundation for the next phase of its digital strategy."

Meg Whitman, Chairman, President, and CEO of Hewlett Packard Enterprise, said, "Deutsche Bank is taking a proactive approach to modernizing its IT infrastructure and has chosen to partner with HP in order to do that. Through this partnership, Deutsche Bank will meet its long-term business objectives through a transformation of its IT infrastructure, including a customized HP Helion solution that will enable them to focus on creating and delivering new services for their clients."

I am seeing more and more CEOs and CFOs becoming particularly frustrated with their IT environments and expenditures. CEOs generally come from finance or sales, not technology, and sometimes they might lack the detailed expertise to completely understand the company's technological issues, so they rely heavily on their CIOs. What they do know is that it is easy for them to use technology as a consumer—so it's hard for them to understand why a company's IT can't work just as simply and smoothly. And the frustration those CEOs feel is understandable. Why can't today's technology enable corporate business functions and processes as easily as the technology we use in our personal lives?

Today I can find an app to do just about anything I can imagine in my personal life. The last time we went sailing, just a few months ago, I decided to experiment with some sailing apps, all of which were readily available on my smartphone—consumption-based software as a service, delivered in the cloud. Sitting in a small bay in Virgin Gorda, British Virgin Islands, I was able to find and install working apps to

- Monitor real-time weather, wind speed, and wave height
- Locate current GPS coordinates and chart waypoints to our next destination, using the most up-to-date marine maps
- Establish real-time distress monitoring in case of accident to automatically notify local search and rescue
- Geo-locate ideal anchor locations, utilizing live earth imagery, with comments and pictures provided by other sailors
- Monitor the boat's water and fuel and predict replenishment needs (The app that made this possible was even able to locate and recommend local marine services and provisioning.)

For peace of mind, I even found an app from ActiveCaptain (see Figure 4-2) that monitored the sailboat's nighttime position for "anchor drag." If the boat moved more than ten meters while anchored, an alarm would sound. Anyone who has sailed and likes to find hidden bays for a great night's sleep will understand the benefit of this app: a good nights sleep. I was able to find and install all these apps within thirty minutes; now *that* is technology as a utility. Meanwhile, as of this writing, I've been waiting four weeks for one of my clients to provide my team with login credentials for a "must have as soon as possible" project!

Figure 4-2 Anchor drag app by ActiveCaptain. (Courtesy of Jeffrey Siegel.)

On a positive note, the CEO will reap much of the benefit of the future mode of operation. CEOs depend on data to solve their companies' problems and get ahead of the curve competitively. This data comes to them both quantitatively and qualitatively. Quantitatively, CEOs receive reports that may indicate problems—reports on increasing day sales outstanding (customers aren't paying their bills on time because they're frustrated); reports that customers are out of stock; reports showing that their manufacturing operations are going down because they lack certain raw materials. CEOs are constantly looking at these metrics—but these metrics are reactive ones: by the time the CEO learns about the problem, it is already happening.

Meanwhile, they are also receiving *qualitative* feedback from their customers in the form of phone calls, e-mails, and text messages—often angry ones.

Traditionally, when these sorts of problems arise, the CEO goes to the CIO and says, "Here's a problem. You have to fix it. What do you need?" And the CIO says, "I can fix this, but I need more hardware. I need more data centers. I need you to give me $30 million to invest in new software." So they start building out their technical capacity internally, and the CEO thinks he is solving the problem.

But in reality, he is making the problem worse. This technical capacity costs time and effort that will ultimately interfere with management's ability to focus on their core competency and proactively look at problems that arise in the business. In addition, this expense has now locked that CEO into an operating model that lacks the flexibility today's market demands. This decision has moved the company from the potential of a continual transformation environment to the reality of inflexibility.

In the future, this is what will happen: a company's technology enablers and many business functions and processes will not be owned by the company at all. Instead, the company will simply pay for the services it needs, using an outcome-based consumption model via partners in the ecosystem.

Let me explain this model using an example. Every company has an order fulfillment, billing, and accounts receivable function. This function of the business is called order to cash (OTC). It is the business process for receiving and processing customer sales from order to cash receipt. A key metric of OTC is "day sales outstanding." Wall Street watches day sales outstanding and cash flow closely and uses these metrics to determine the valuation of a company. Because of this scrutiny, a CFO is always asking, "From the time an order is received, how long does it take to collect money for that invoice? And how can we make that time as short as possible?"

If a company has a problem with day sales outstanding, the CEO, CFO, and CIO will confer and try to rectify the problem. Under the current mode of operation, the CIO might ask for millions of dollars to install upgrades on the SAP accounts receivable and collections software and buy more servers, and finance might want to hire more accounts receivable clerks and collection agents. In return for this investment, the CIO and CFO may promise to reduce the day sales outstanding from forty-two days to thirty-six days. Maybe the plan will work, and maybe it won't, but either way, the company will now be yoked to expensive IT software and infrastructure, and more inflexible headcount and payroll expense

In the future, the CEO and the rest of the leadership team will be aware that the company's core competency is not generating invoices and collecting money, nor is it the buying and installation of the technology associated with generating invoices and collecting money. This is not where they should be spending their money or their management energy.

Instead, the company of the future will have its *ecosystem*—that is, a company or series of companies—handle its order to cash (OTC). The company will pay its ecosystem provider based on a promised outcome—say, when day sales outstanding moves from forty-two days to fifteen days. The CEO and the rest of the management team will not care which technology enablers their partner uses—they won't have any meetings about hardware or software—because that's not their problem to solve anymore. This full solution technology/ business process service partner will utilize its own technology enablers and will bring its own accounts receivable clerks and collection agents as needed. This will all work seamlessly, powered by the convergence of technology in cloud, mobile, SaaS, and data. Why? This trusted partner in the ecosystem has a core competency in OTC and is linked into the continual transformation environment operating model of its client.

For example, a company might partner with Hewlett Packard Enterprise, using a very simple contract. HP would handle everything from the time an order is placed—in other words, all of the processes associated with invoice generation and collection once the goods exit the facility.

Hewlett Packard Enterprise would charge the company based on an outcome—such as achieving day sales outstanding of fifteen days. So all the meetings a chief financial officer would otherwise need to have in order to select the right technology, to assess the proper technical requirements, to install the right technology hardware and software, and to hire the right account receivable clerks and collection clerks would be unnecessary. The partner would have all those meetings internally. It would be HP's responsibility to do whatever it needed to do to bring the day sales outstanding down to fifteen days—or not get paid.

In this future, Hewlett Packard Enterprise would be one company in an ecosystem of partners that collaborate with the main client in that company's product value chain. Each company in the ecosystem would bring its core competency to the value chain. At the core of the ecosystem is the main client company, which can concentrate on its core competency and competitive advantage strategies. And each partner company in the ecosystem would be paid based on the outcome of the service it provided.

The idea of outsourcing a company's nonessential functions in order to focus on core competency is not new. Companies in the past outsourced certain functions for *comparative advantage*—a term used by economists to describe a situation in which other firms can provide that function or service at lower marginal cost. Today we must move our non-core functions to our ecosystem for *competitive advantage*. What is new is the fanatical focus on core competency, which forces non-core competency activities into the ecosystem, thus creating a continual transformation environment operating model.

It is the convergence of key technology trends and enablers that brings the ecosystem to reality and thus enables the continual transformation environment. The emergence of cloud, mobility, software as a service, and data allows true consumption-based IT; payment can be based on IT consumption or business outcome. All the companies in the ecosystem bring their own technologies to the relationship, and because of this convergence, all the technologies can be interoperable. This will allow all the partnered companies to take their efficiencies to new, previously unseen levels.

Newco Versus Oldco

A new company (Newco) is much more able to embrace this core-competency-driven ecosystem and value chain than an older company (Oldco). Oldco companies tend to be encumbered: they've spent many years investing in data centers, computer hardware, and software, and they've spent millions on custom programming and systems integration. Structural and attitudinal rigidity often result because it's hard to walk away from that kind of investment.

A Newco, on the other hand, is unencumbered. Within months of starting up, it can have infrastructure equal to that of a global multibillion-dollar company through the use of the ecosystem. Such a company can partner with Salesforce.com for customer relationship management, or Workday.com for human resources management, or Hewlett Packard for finance and accounting and supply-chain management. A Newco can assemble an entire ecosystem almost instantly because it is not encumbered by old ways of thinking.

For example, look at Instagram, an online social networking service for mobile photo and video sharing. Instagram launched in October 2010 and was acquired by Facebook in 2012 for $1 billion; by 2014, it had more than 300 million users.

Had Instagram launched twenty years ago, it would have built data centers around the globe and leased a global fiber-optic network to handle its traffic. It would have developed its own sales force, its own payroll department, its own human resources department, its own accounts payable department, and so on.

But it didn't need to do these things. When it launched in 2010, Instagram didn't invest in servers or infrastructure. Instead, it established an ecosystem of providers, including Amazon Web Services, to provide the necessary infrastructure. Other companies followed similar paths. Snapchat was built using Google's cloud services. Facebook for years did not own any of its own data centers; instead, it had a large ecosystem of partners. Those companies concentrated on their core competencies and let their ecosystem of partners handle the rest. From the beginning, Facebook had a fanatical focus on its vision—their core competency. This is where it spent its management bandwidth and its capital assets. What Instagram, Snapchat and Facebook built through its ecosystem in a few years, Oldco is still resisting.

Return on Invested Capital

Wall Street increasingly wants older companies to emulate newer companies like Facebook or Uber in their ability to increase return on invested capital (ROIC). ROIC is net operating profit minus taxes minus dividends divided by invested capital:

$$\text{ROIC} = \frac{Net\ Operating\ Profit - Adjusted\ Taxes - Dividend}{Invested\ Capital}$$

To explore ROIC, I want to use the example of a certain newspaper company. This particular newspaper does $1 billion of revenue and makes $200 million in pre-tax profit. It owns its own printing presses. It has invested $100 million in printing presses, and that $100 million is amortized over ten years, giving the company a $10 million capital depreciation expense every year. So, the company has $100 million of assets and generates $200 million in profit before depreciation expense. This is the newspaper's current mode of operation. As newspaper subscribers convert from the print product to digital, the newspaper will continue to have that same printing press asset on its books, and the cash that was used for that asset is out of the bank.

In the newspaper's future mode of operation, it won't own its printing presses, so those won't be valued as a company asset, and the company will keep that $100 million in its coffers. It will still have $1 billion in revenue and $200 million in pre-tax profits. It will spend $10 million (currently on the books under depreciation expense for a capital expense, or CAPEX) on a service provider to print the paper. And it will still generate $200 million of profit—but in this scenario, it will be able to generate this profit *without needing to invest in any assets*.

And as consumers shift from the print product to digital subscriptions, the newspaper's expense (being consumption-based) will decrease. It will have started on a path toward a core competency-based, continual transformation environment.

It's easy to see how this model is appealing to an investor.

In old companies, more capital assets are needed to generate the same profit. Wall Street looks at this ROIC metric and says to an old company, "Why are you tying up your money—or my money!—in all these assets? You're tying up money in assets that aren't related to your core competency, and you're lowering your ROIC. You could perform the same business function with an ecosystem of providers on a consumption model and use the money you would have tied up in capital assets for innovation, acquisitions, or even dividends back to me!"

In my personal stock portfolio, I look at how companies are generating cash flow and on what level of fixed assets. I look very specifically at their return on invested capital relative to their trailing and forward-looking net operating profit. I also look at the companies that, in my opinion, are concentrating on their core competencies. If their ROIC is going up, then this is a company that is shedding its non-core competency assets. The company gets it. It is preparing for the future. I personally only invest in companies with a fanatical emphasis on their core competency, a robust ecosystem of partners handling their non-core activities, and a growing cash flow on a low asset base. A good ROIC that is continuing to improve is paramount. For calendar 2014, my individual brokerage account had a one-year return of 53.05%. Through June 2015, my year-to-date return was 49.51%.

Most companies don't spend enough energy on ROIC. They tend to focus instead on another metric: EBITDA (which stands for earnings before interest, taxes, depreciation, and amortization). But, as described next, a 2011 *Forbes* article offered five reasons why EBITDA is increasingly questionable as a financial performance and value indicator.

EBITDA makes companies with asset-heavy balance sheets appear to be healthier than they may actually be.

Understanding the amount of asset depreciation is of little value when attempting to determine a company's current viability; it's a measure of the company's past spending on capital expenditures. As "non-cash" items, depreciation and amortization are meaningless in the context of a company's future fiscal health.

EBITDA indicates a company's debt service ability—but only some types of debt.

EBITDA helps investment bankers determine how much debt a buyer can put on a company after it's acquired, although just how well it answers that question depends on the type of debt held by a creditor—in other words, whether the creditor's position is advantageous or highly precarious. So unless you're the senior secured lender and the EBITDA number exceeds your debt service for the period projected, EBITDA has little practical value.

EBITDA ignores working capital requirements.

If you own a chain of retail stores and it's June, then like many other retail chains whose sales are more robust during the holidays, your company's year-to-date EBITDA may be positive, and your cash operations may be flirting with breakeven, if not showing outright losses.

Your positive EBITDA doesn't reflect your true cash position and financial health because it's June, and you have to start ordering for the holiday season, which means cash tied up in inventory—cash you don't have. So either you have to borrow more, which increases debt service costs, or you have to use what cash is on hand and do what the trade credit community calls "stretching payables."

Either way, EBITDA doesn't reflect changes in working capital requirements.

EBITDA doesn't adhere to GAAP.

The Generally Accepted Accounting Principles (GAAP) are the hallmark of transparency and consistency in financial reporting. Because EBITDA is essentially a tool that shows what a company would look like if it weren't actually that company, it is easily manipulated. EBITDA also doesn't provide any consistency check for a company's accounting practices—that is, how it arrives at its cash flow reporting.

EBITDA can present a laundry list of bad information.

In 2000, Moody's Investors Services released a report titled "Ten Critical Failings of EBITDA as the Principal Determinant of Cash Flow." According to this report, those who use EBITDA as the sole basis for determination of a transaction multiple likely deserve the results they get. While EBITDA multiples are some of many transaction multiples that need to be considered when calculating the purchase price of a business, there are numerous better ones to use—particularly when EBITDA is so easily manipulated.

Stick with cash flow and ROIC. You will thank me at retirement.

Presumption Must Be No Owned IT Assets

Thanks to the convergence of technologies—the cloud, mobility, SaaS, and data—companies now have the ability to create partner ecosystems that allow them to concentrate on their core competencies. This in turn improves their ROIC from a financial metric point of view. They can now handle all their business functions without the burdensome expense of inflexible assets.

With this in mind, I definitely state that a company should never purchase IT hardware or software licenses again. Period. Every time a company makes a software purchase, a computer purchase—a server, storage, a workstation, a tablet, or a notebook—it is wasting the shareholders' money. By buying that piece of equipment, the company has entered into a never-ending capital expense cycle because a computer starts becoming obsolete the minute it's bought. The company will replace that same hardware in four years, or it'll be stuck working on obsolete hardware, which is a competitive disadvantage.

The same is true every time the company makes a software license purchase and enters into a software maintenance agreement. It is wasting the shareholders' money. In addition, the company hurts its balance sheet by bringing on assets that negatively affect ROIC. It has ignored its core competency and created an inflexible situation, thereby denying itself a continual transformation environment.

In the future, a company will look to its CTE ecosystem to provide the technology enablers it needs on a consumption basis. When an employee needs a workstation or a laptop, it also will be provided by the CTE ecosystem on a consumption basis. Companies will partner with organizations like HP, which will provide laptops, tablets, or workstations on a consumption-based model. For example, a company may receive a laptop for $10 a month per employee, and then, once every twenty-four months or so, replace that laptop with a new one that has the newest technology on it. Companies like HP can do this because laptops are part of HP's core competency. So are data centers and the cloud. So is keeping up on the latest software, hardware, processes, and security governance. HP focuses on its core competency and provides services to its partner companies so that they are free to stop thinking about IT and can focus on their core competencies and competitive advantage.

Control and Fear

So why are so many companies afraid to enter into partnerships with companies that have the core competencies they need? From my viewpoint as a consultant, it comes down to control and fear. Companies worry about what happens if there is a catastrophic loss. They wonder what would happen, for example, if their cloud-based technology infrastructure suddenly shut down. Companies fear that they will become powerless; that in the event of catastrophe, their business will falter, and they won't be able to do anything but call an 800 number and complain.

But again, this comes back to core competency. Who is more likely to have a tested disaster recovery system—a company whose core competency is totally focused on IT, or a company with a local IT department and a non-IT core competency?

In most companies, the CIO needs to be relieved of the responsibility for building and running IT. Instead, the CIO needs to focus on doing what it takes to develop an ecosystem of partners dedicated to the core competencies and business enablers that the company does not have, including IT. That means the CIO needs to transform the IT department into a service broker, setting the architecture, governance, and standards to govern the company's whole ecosystem as a service broker for outcome-based business enablers. Once established, these standards become the criteria for finding partners. The

CIO's defining role is building a world-class ecosystem that complements the company's core competency and provides the flexibility of a continual transformation environment.

It is the convergence of technology trends in cloud, mobility, software as a service, and data that is allowing companies to move to the continual transformation environment ecosystem. So, let's now take a look at each of these technology areas and its impact.

Divestiture Provides Del Monte Opportunity for Continual Transformation Environment

New companies have an advantage over older more established companies. They do not have the structural or attitudinal inherencies blocking them from moving to the continual transformation environment that will allow for competitive advantage. For Del Monte, a divestiture gave the company the impetus it needed for true transformational change.

First used in the 1880s, the Del Monte brand is one of the oldest in the world—as well as one of the most-recognized and best-loved. Not long ago, however, some naysayers wondered if the privately owned U.S. company that originated the Del Monte brand would be able to survive. The crisis was precipitated by a divestiture. For nearly a decade, Del Monte Foods, Inc. (DMFI) was known as Del Monte Corporation, and its portfolio included both human food and pet food products. Then the company's owners decided to focus on the pet food division and put the DMFI portion of the company up for sale.

It found a buyer: the Manila-based Del Monte Pacific, which licenses the Del Monte name. But the sale presented DMFI with a daunting challenge: it lost both its IT infrastructure and its back office organization. To survive, DMFI had only one choice: it had to build out both of those critical operational components from the ground up—and it had less than a year to do it. DMFI met that challenge with the help of its strategic business partner, HP.

"It was about rebirth." So begins Timothy Weaver, CIO for DMFI, as he reflects on the challenges the company faced after the divestiture. "We realized we could leverage the split as an opportunity to reinvent ourselves," Weaver says. "It was an opportunity to take our company, which has a rich history and all the traditional strengths of a well-respected brand, and adopt a completely new way of doing business."

Weaver and the other DMFI executives had a vision for what a reinvented DMFI would look like. "Every functional area of our organization had its own business process platform," says David Withycombe, COO for DMFI. "We needed a way to bring everyone together so that operationally we'd be working from a single set of facts and working toward a single, common purpose." "We were holding our legacy systems together with duct tape and baling twine," Weaver says. "We wanted to replace that with a modern, enterprise SAP platform." In terms of technology, DMFI also wanted to move to cloud-based architecture. "We announced a cloud-only strategy," Weaver continues. "We knew that cloud would help us remain lean and would give us the ability to move more quickly as a business."

Outsourcing was the final piece of the vision. DMFI had a previous outsourcing relationship with HP; with the divestiture, it made sense to review outsourcing options again. "We didn't want to build IT or business process optimization expertise in-house," Weaver explains. "And we didn't want to add a whole new accounting team. Outsourcing those functions lets us focus on our business, our customers, and what helps us succeed in the marketplace."

Outsourcing also conferred another potential benefit. It would let DMFI ramp up resources if necessary. And it was definitely necessary. When the sale of DMFI was finalized, the company signed a temporary services agreement (TSA); under the terms of the TSA, DMFI could continue to use the IT infrastructure and back office resources that were remaining with the pet foods division. But the TSA expired in a year and was not considered renewable. If DMFI didn't succeed in implementing a new IT platform in time, it would lose access to almost 400 business applications and tools that it needed to run its operations. And not everybody thought that a year was enough. "We had consultants come in and tell us, 'good luck, but you don't have a prayer,'" recalls Gene Allen, SVP Business Transformation for DMFI. But Allen, who joined the company to steer it through the post-sale waters, never doubted that DMFI had what it took to not only survive, but thrive. "We knew it was possible. We just didn't know how to do it. We needed a partner—someone we could trust, who had expertise in the right areas."

So DMFI engaged HP to do two things: build out, manage, and support a new, cloud-based SAP infrastructure; and build out and staff an outsourced Finance and Administration (F&A) organization. Normally, a project of this scale would take at least 18 months, but in this case, DMFI needed the build-out and migration completed in only 8. With only 8 months to complete an 18-month project, HP had to move fast. And there was a prodigious amount of work to be done. The team had to architect and implement a completely new IT infrastructure. It had to deploy SAP core financials, including extended warehouse management, quality management, and customer relationship management/trade promotion management. It had to define entirely new back office processes and create a new F&A organization to manage them.

"With HP's help, we ran a marathon at a sprinter's pace," says Weaver.

Close to 400 point applications had to be rationalized and targeted for upgrade or retirement. Siloes that had built up over years or decades had to be torn down. People accustomed to working in certain ways had to start learning new work habits and processes. To make it happen, HP Enterprise Services drew on its broad portfolio of solutions and services to transform Del Monte's application and infrastructure.

DMFI and HP built, tested, and implemented a cloud-based IT infrastructure hosted in an HP Helion Virtual Private Cloud data center in Tulsa, Oklahoma, on a mix of Microsoft Windows 2012 and Linux Red Hat physical and virtual servers. They installed SAP and established backup and disaster recovery processes, leveraging the HP Helion Continuity solution to reduce the risk of business outages. They set up and cut over all DMFI sites to their new WAN/LAN and phone systems, and deployed new HP laptops and desktops to all DMFI employees.

Concurrently, HP also transitioned DMFI's F&A processes to an HP Business Process Services team. DMFI and HP first defined the SAP-based processes required to support critical F&A services through a blueprint phase, which included record-to-report, accounts payable, and accounts receivable. They selected and implemented the SAP modules needed to support those processes. Then they performed the knowledge transfer and handover to ensure that the new F&A team would be ready to support DMFI after the SAP cutover.

Throughout the project, DMFI and HP worked as a single team. "It was a shared commitment," Allen says. "If you stepped into one of our meetings, you would not have known who was from HP and who was from DMFI." And while the demands of the project were substantial—members of both companies often worked 12 to 16 hour days, seven days a week—the commitment paid off. The new SAP platform and F&A processes were up and running by the project deadline. There was zero disruption to DMFI's customers during the transition.

"HP delivered against every objective they set out to deliver against," says Withycombe.

Meeting the deadline benefited DMFI in a number of ways. It laid to rest any questions about the company's future. It energized DMFI's executives, investors, and employees, because they all knew, with absolute confidence, that the company was embarking on an exciting new chapter. And on a more practical level, it accelerated the real-world benefits of the new platform and processes.

Once the new SAP platform and processes were in place, DMFI turned its attention to the other components of its transformation: stabilizing the business, optimizing its new processes, and managing change. As the company moves forward on its new IT infrastructure, it will increasingly realize a number of improvements across its IT and business processes. Whereas the old infrastructure was dated and prone to issues and outages, the new virtual private cloud platform delivers 99.9% availability. DMFI's data is better-protected, thanks to built-in system redundancy and backup processes that conform to industry best practices.

The implementation simplified the company's environment, reducing the number of business applications from approximately 400 to approximately 70. Processes are more efficient. Before, data often had to be entered manually into multiple systems. Now, it can be entered once; the SAP applications automatically feed the data to whatever applications require it. Processes that once took up to 20 discrete steps can now be completed with a single mouse click.

The business is no longer siloed. "The SAP platform integrates our business across all operational areas," Weaver notes. "Immediately after implementation, we began seeing more and better collaboration. And we now have a consolidated view of how our business operates. We're better able to manage dependencies fundamental to our business, like ensuring that our supply matches demand, and that promotional activities are tied appropriately to both."

The transformation also delivers cost savings. HP and DMFI cited the new F&A organization within DMFI's parent company in the Philippines, for example—an elegant way to leverage a mix of offshore and on-shore resources to keep costs down. The new cloud infrastructure and the efficiencies delivered by the SAP implementation will keep DMFI's long-term operational costs in check and aligned to the business. This, in turn, will enable the company to invest more of its cash in strategic programs that drive growth and market share.

At the same time, however, the company's market is a mature one. While DMFI can't put its brand at risk by compromising on quality, it must keep its products price-competitive. By enabling both process improvements and cost containment, DMFI's new cloud infrastructure, SAP applications, and F&A organization will help the company to achieve those potentially conflicting objectives.

The real winners are the consumers. Because DMFI has a better handle on its operational processes, for example, it can precisely coordinate its production, inventory, supply chain, and promotions. So when a working mother clips a Sunday coupon for a DMFI product, she can trust that product will be on the shelf of her favorite grocery store the next time she shops.

"Most consumers don't think about what it takes, in today's world, to bring all of the elements together that they expect from Del Monte products: the quality, the safety, the cost," Withycombe explains. "Now, we can go to one screen to view and manage all of those elements with a click of a button."

"This project demonstrates that DMFI is committed to the future. Not only do we believe in our own people, but we partnered with the right organization in HP to drive this company to new levels of success," says Withycombe.

"Ultimately, our strategy resolves to meeting our customers' needs," notes David L. Meyers, Chief Financial Officer for DMFI. "By helping us achieve this business transformation, HP has positioned us to pinpoint our attention and resources on delighting consumers who know and love the Del Monte brand. And there is nothing more important to us than that."

5   Cloud Computing

Cloud computing is a major technology trend that has perme-ated the market over the last two years. It sets the stage for a new approach to IT that enables individuals and businesses to choose how they'll acquire or deliver IT services, with reduced emphasis on the constraints of traditional software and hardware licensing models. Cloud computing has a sig-nificant potential impact on every aspect of IT and how users access applications, information, and business services.

—David W. Cearley, VP & Gartner Fellow, Gartner Inc.

Not too long ago, I held the title "household CIO," meaning that under that old mode of operation, I built and ran the IT department in my home. If computers or printers needed to be hooked up, or software needed to be installed on a computer, the job fell to me.

And it really was a job. I devoted several hours per week to ensuring that every computer in the house was up and running. I had to buy hardware and software for the computers, printers, and network, and when the network went down (which happened frequently), I had to troubleshoot until everyone was back online and fully functioning again.

The more IT-enabled appliances (such as smartphones) came into the household, the more I had to do as household CIO. I reluctantly accepted the title, and my job was to build and run that home network. Does this feel familiar?

Fast forward to 2015. I am still the household CIO, but I no longer build and run a network for my home. Nobody in the family (including me) even thinks of the network anymore. The amount of time I spend as the household CIO is virtually zero. Why? Because of the consumerization of IT. Now everything is automatically connected and working. My wife and son go to the Apple or Google app store and automatically download any application they need right onto their laptop or tablet. Within minutes, that application is up and running. The days of me having to go to the computer store to buy software are over.

Our phones are a part of this, too. They automatically join the network as soon as they are in range of the house. The only thing they require is a password. Say we add a printer or a new computer. We take it out of the box, turn it on, and it immediately asks for the network name and password. We enter that info, and we're up and running. As for interoperability, my accounting program talks to my bank account, which talks to my tax preparation program. No need for massive IT integration work.

We don't spend nearly as much time maintaining and building the home network as we used to because everything has been consumerized. It is a utility. Our home computer network today is very much like our electrical service or our gas service. We flip a switch, and it's on. We need e-mail, and there it is. Do we need a new social media application? We go to the app store and download it. There is now quite a long list of technology-driven processes in our household that do not require an IT technician (or the household CIO): annual taxes, household accounting, retirement planning, personal e-mail and collaboration, social networking, education, entertainment, and even our household supply-chain management (i.e., groceries and household items inventory and just-in-time replenishment). All of this IT has been consumerized and is simply utilized by our family, much like the other utilities we use in our household.

I think a lot of people can relate to the way it used to be, the frustration many people felt when they faced problems with IT at home: "My computer's down." "I need new software—can you go buy it for me?" "I have a new game I'd like you to install." "The printer doesn't work." "My computer is infected by a virus." How many hours did we spend building and running our home networks? That was only a few years ago. And now that's just gone. At home, everything really is utility based. I haven't bought software at a store in quite some time, and there is a good chance I never will again, whereas the previous model required me to go out and buy new software (and hardware) many times during the year.

Shouldn't corporate IT work the same way? It will. The IT in our personal lives is so consumerized and easy to use that we now demand the same ease of use in our professional lives. And there is no reason not to. Personal IT has become so easy to use that business users have started changing employment when companies do not provide the type of user experience in the office that they have in their personal life. A 2011 Accenture Survey revealed that 45 percent of respondents believed their personal consumer devices were more useful than the tools and applications provided by their employers. Twenty-seven percent of those surveyed were even willing to pay for their own devices to use at work because of the improvement in productivity and job satisfaction.

"Employees feel increasingly empowered to make their own technology decisions and say that corporate IT is just not as flexible and convenient as the personal consumer devices and software applications they use in their personal lives," states Jeanne Harris, executive research fellow and senior executive at the Accenture Institute for High Performance. The Accenture study also uncovered that 88 percent of executives surveyed linked employee use of consumer technology with improved job satisfaction. Unfortunately, corporate America has not made a lot of headway in providing that consumerized

IT experience for its business users since this study was conducted in 2011.

When I first talk with the leadership teams of the companies that hire me, I make the bold statement provided in an earlier chapter: I tell them that they should never buy hardware or software again. Period.

Every time a company makes a computer hardware purchase—a server, workstation, tablet, or notebook—it is wasting shareholder money and diminishing the chance that the company will stay focused on its core competency. This will prevent the company from creating a continual transformation environment that will provide the flexibility necessary to ensure competitive advantage. Every server it owns will be obsolete within a few years. By the time the capital budget is available to replace the servers, employees will be working on old hardware and systems, putting the company at a competitive disadvantage. In addition, by buying IT hardware, the company commits to a never-ending capital expense and creates declining value on a key metric of its valuation, ROIC.

The mantra I want my clients to repeat is, "We don't need to purchase hardware because we are moving everything to the cloud!" It might be Amazon's cloud, or Hewlett Packard's cloud, or Microsoft's cloud, or Google's cloud or more than likely a combination of several partners' clouds; what Hewlett Packard Enterprise calls the converged cloud. The end result is the same: we are out of the business of owning and running data centers and purchasing hardware and software.

We don't need to buy servers because the technology partners in our CTE ecosystem provide us what we need in their clouds. They will provide their services on a pure consumption basis, as we need them. Hardware and software in the cloud are automatically upgraded as technology is introduced. The upgrades are so seamless that we never see or notice them. Like magic, we are always working on the most technologically current system.

CIOs need to accept the fact that the idea of owning or leasing a data center is obsolete. To ensure competitive advantage, it is time to stop buying data center assets and start placing all of our IT workloads in the cloud.

It seems obvious to me that my clients should immediately switch to the cloud. But cloud computing technology is still such a new way of thinking that people often have to overcome obstacles in their own thinking before they will consider implementing it. I have been in countless meetings with CIOs debating the meanings of various terms: What is a cloud? What is "cloud-like"? What is a "public cloud" versus a "private cloud" versus a "virtual private cloud"? This is a perfect example of wasted management attention and bandwidth; only the very few senior IT architects who must make those decisions need to worry about these things.

What matters to me and should matter to you is the outcome. Companies must make applications and data available through a consumption-based infrastructure that will function regardless of geographic location or method of distribution. As illustrated in Figure 5-1, if employees have mobile phones or tablets or notebooks, they should have easy access to the software applications they need. Employees don't need to know if their applications and data are distributed on a large public cloud such as Google, or Hewlett Packard's virtual private cloud, or Amazon's very basic public cloud. They just need access to the applications and data they need to do their work.

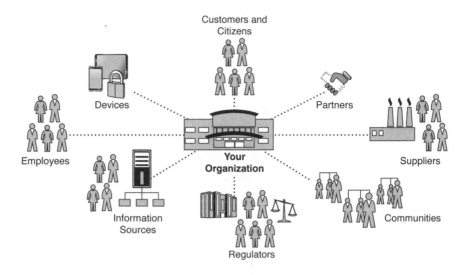

Figure 5-1 The cloud enables connectivity of your eco-system, regardless of geography or device.

Companies need to think of computing as a utility, which requires cloud or cloud-like infrastructure and payment mechanisms. Virtually every country and corner of the globe is now connected through consumption-based networked infrastructures. Yes, someone does own the data centers and fiber optic networks and servers and SANs that keep it all running. However, the key takeaway is that companies do not need to own and provide this cloud technology to themselves. Doing so is not their core competency, and they must rely on their CTE eco-system to provide it to their business users.

For example, when the entrepreneurs who started Instagram wanted to deliver data and images to Singapore, Hong Kong, Mumbai, Frankfurt, New York City, Los Angeles, and Sydney, they created a software-defined network in a cloud. That became the Instagram network. They pay for the network only when they use it. They didn't have to buy servers or data centers or network infrastructure. Literally, within twenty-four hours of calling their service provider and saying, "I need a network capable of reaching the five corners of the Earth," they had one.

Other notable companies that use mostly consumption-based cloud or cloud-like services include Procter & Gamble, Netflix, Pinterest, and Heroku, just to name a few. In today's world, a company can place its workloads and utilize IT infrastructure in more than 190 countries without owning a single server themselves.

What Is Cloud Computing?

In cloud computing, a company does not know—or need to know—where its server resides or the capacity of that server. Let's say I want to run a report that requires a little more computing power than I have in my office. I don't know if the report's running on a server in Tulsa or New York or Finland. All I know is that it's running. The cloud instantly knows if it needs more central processing units (CPUs) or more storage, and it provides it. This is commonly referred to as *elasticity*, which Wikipedia defines as "the degree to which a system is able to adapt to workload changes by provisioning and deprovisioning resources in an autonomic manner, such that at each point in time the available resources match the current demand as closely as possible."

Under the CTE operating model, the IT department of the future will not build and run IT infrastructure, platforms, and applications. However, it *will* set architecture and governance standards for its ecosystem of providers. Management should not have to expend valuable time and effort determining how technology enablers will be provided—although a small group of individuals within the IT business unit must establish the architectural standards for how the ecosystem integrates. With that in mind, a fundamental definition of cloud computing is necessary.

The National Institute of Standards and Technology (NIST) defines cloud computing like this: "Cloud computing is a model for enabling ubiquitous, convenient, on-demand network access to a shared pool of configurable computing resources (e.g., networks, servers, storage, applications, and services) that can be rapidly provisioned and released with minimal management effort or service provider interaction." NIST goes on to describe five essential characteristics of cloud computing:

- **On-demand self-service**—A consumer can provision computing capabilities automatically as needed, without needing to interact with the human agents of each service provider.

- **Broad network access**—Capabilities are available over the network and accessed through various client platforms (e.g., workstations, laptops, tablets, and mobile phones).

- **Resource pooling**—The provider pools its computing resources in order to serve multiple consumers using a multi-tenant model, dynamically assigning and reassigning physical and virtual resources according to consumer demand. The customer generally does not know the exact location of the provided resources, but he or she may be able to specify location at a higher level of abstraction (e.g., country, state, or data center). Examples of resources include storage, processing, memory, and network bandwidth.

- **Rapid elasticity**—Capabilities can be elastically provisioned and released—in some cases automatically—to scale rapidly outward and inward according to demand.

- **Measured service**—Cloud systems automatically control and optimize resource use by leveraging a metering capability at some level of abstraction appropriate to the type of service (e.g., storage, processing, bandwidth, and active user accounts). The use of resources can be monitored, controlled, and reported, providing transparency for both the provider and the consumer.

Why the Cloud?

The fact that the definition of the term *cloud* is subject to such heated debate somewhat supports the thesis that companies and management are spending too much time on the *how* and not enough on the *outcome*. The outcome is an absolute necessity in our increasingly demanding business environment; companies must have a continual transformation environment that ensures flexibility and prevents a company from being "locked in" to a strategy, tactic, cost, process, or location. The outcome must be so flexible that a firm can sunset an operation, function, process, or location in a matter of weeks (or days) without any financial setback. In the same manner, a company must be able to initiate new operations, functions, processes, or locations in the same time frame.

Advantages for companies that have cloud-based IT include:

- Access to data from anywhere, at any time (as with e-mail), using an ordinary Internet connection
- Relief from the stress of buying software licenses for every tool they install
- Elimination of hardware costs (because apps and data are stored and copied on the cloud)
- Reduced processing-power requirements for their end user computers (without reduction in performance)
- Money saved on IT support, server maintenance, and data storage space
- Solving complex problems quickly and easily by using a grid of cloud computers instead of a single personal computer
- Ability to grow a business at its own pace, without stressing systems as customer bases grow

- Lower costs (You pay for cloud services based on the consumption you use—like taxi fares. And like a taxi, the meter stops running as soon as you stop using the cloud.)

Under the cloud computing umbrella, there are different types of cloud deployment models, as shown in Figure 5-2. The IT department of the future as a service broker of their ecosystem of providers will set architecture and standards for integration and interoperability. This will allow the company to operate seamlessly from a technology standpoint while utilizing different types of cloud deployment models. HP refers to this as the *converged cloud model*.

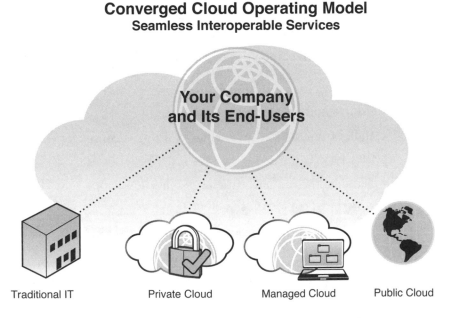

Figure 5-2 Cloud deployment models vary and most companies will utilize them all.

Cloud Deployment Models

People get caught up in whether a service is a true cloud or "cloud-like." Don't worry about that! Just focus on your employees being able to access a service anywhere in the world, for a small price per consumption, from a company whose core competency is to run the underlying infrastructure. We don't need to be naïve—yes, there are technical considerations and decisions—but CEOs and CIOs must first embrace the outcome. They then must mandate that the company be 100 percent consumption based by a certain date.

The small group of individuals who need to make decisions about transferring workloads to the cloud will be looking at three primary cloud deployment models: public cloud, private cloud, and managed (or virtual private) cloud. Understanding that there are different types of cloud deployments, the company must embrace a converged cloud operating model (CCOM) that makes the underlying cloud deployment model used for specific workloads opaque to the business user. Remember, to the business user, we are implementing a utility model: flip the switch, and the light goes on. While it may (and should) matter to a select few in the IT department whether an application is deployed on a public, private, or virtual private cloud, this should be opaque and meaningless to the business user.

So in general, how are these deployment models different from one another, and what are the typical workloads that will use each deployment model?

- **Public cloud**—For most consumers, the most recognizable model of cloud computing is the public cloud model, which provides cloud services in a virtual environment that uses shared physical resources and is accessible over a public network—usually the Internet. The public cloud differs from private clouds—which are accessible only for a single organization—in that it uses a single shared infrastructure to provide services to multiple clients. Generally, public cloud environments are the most cost-effective, but they should be used for workloads that do not have extremely sensitive data and for those that have lower service-level requirements. Typical uses for public clouds include e-mail, messaging, and other office and noncritical applications.

- **Private cloud**—Private cloud infrastructure is for the *exclusive* use of a single organization. Private clouds are well suited for mission-critical applications with high service-level requirements and applications with sensitive data, including personally identifiable information (PII) data and protected health information data (such as that covered by the Health Insurance Portability and Accountability Act [HIPAA]).

- **Virtual private cloud (VPC), or managed cloud**—A VPC is a cloud computing service offered by a cloud provider that sets aside a portion of its public cloud infrastructure for private use. A public cloud provider manages the infrastructure of a VPC, but the resources allocated to it are not shared with the provider's other customers. This model is ideally suited to critical enterprise resource planning applications such as finance and human resources.

- **Converged cloud operating model (CCOM)**—Key aspects of the utility delivery model are a seamless user experience, interoperability and unified management. Determining what workloads are delivered by what cloud deployment models will be a key role of the IT business unit of the future. However, once that architecture is put into place, the day-to-day usage and delivery of applications should be absolutely seamless to the end user. In a converged cloud operating model, workloads are governed and managed on a common architecture that spans the three deployment models (and even an interim deployment model that includes traditional IT). The end result is one layer of interoperable services and unified management for all workloads regardless of where deployed. This is a critical aspect of the new role of the IT business unit as a service broker.

Compare these cloud deployment models to the current ways of doing things. If you were working with a traditional data center, you would know that it was physically located at a specific physical address and that it has a hundred servers with four hundred CPUs and three hundred twenty terabytes of storage. You purchase and refresh this hardware every four to five years. In daily use, when a CPU or the storage maxes out, your program crashes. In a cloud environment, however, you do not buy any hardware. If your workload expands, the cloud recognizes this expansion in real time and provides more CPUs and storage. If the workload decreases, the cloud downsizes the infrastructure, and you are charged appropriately. You face no capital expenditures, no expense related to being over capacity, and no risk of system outages related to being under capacity. I contend that every company must move its entire application stack and IT infrastructure to cloud deployments if they wish to ensure competitive advantage.

Now, we need to understand that until we reach the future mode of operation, there will be temporary modes of operation. Application transformation to the cloud is a journey. During this journey, companies will most likely have applications on four deployment models: traditional, public, managed, and private. And, in some very rare instances, companies for absolutely critical reasons may decide to keep a limited number of applications on a traditional IT platform. What needs to be emphasized is that *the presumption must always be to have your applications running in the cloud*. The bar must be set very high if an IT department desires to keep an application in a traditional IT deployment model.

Within the cloud deployment models, different types of service models are needed for both business and IT users, and these service models can be deployed on each of the deployment models described, depending on requirements. These service models are:

- **Software as a service (SaaS)**—SaaS enables a business user to run the provider's applications on a cloud, usually on a pay-per-use basis. The applications can be accessed either through a thin client interface such as a web browser (e.g., web-based e-mail) or via a program interface. The consumer does not manage the underlying cloud infrastructure, except possibly for a few user-specific application configuration settings. The enterprise market, like the consumer market, will soon be dominated by SaaS offerings to business users, who will access these applications via the enterprise app store (see Chapter 7, "SaaS and the Enterprise App Store").

- **Platform as a service (PaaS)**—PaaS enables a business user to deploy onto the cloud infrastructure applications acquired or created by the business using programming languages, services, and tools supported by the provider. The business user does not manage the underlying cloud infrastructure but has control over the deployed applications and may also control configuration settings for the application-hosting environment. IT business units that create their own applications will use PaaS to deploy those applications to business users.

- **Infrastructure as a service (IaaS)**—IaaS enables the user to provision CPUs, storage, networks, and other fundamental computing resources to deploy and run arbitrary software, such as operating systems and applications. The user does not manage or control the underlying cloud infrastructure but has control over operating systems, storage, and deployed applications; the user may also have limited control of select networking components (e.g., host firewalls). IaaS is not needed by the typical business user and will only be used by IT business unit staff in limited situations, as the market becomes dominated by SaaS.

Cloud computing deployment models and SaaS service models are now widely used in the consumer apps world. Examples of this include personal e-mail such as Gmail, social applications such as LinkedIn and Facebook, and personal finance programs such as Mint. Most of our consumer tools are cloud based, and most of our business tools soon will be. Many already are, including Salesforce.com for customer relationship management and Workday.com for human resource management.

Some companies don't share my enthusiasm for the cloud and aren't moving quickly enough to take advantage of it. To some degree, the problem stems from an attitude shared by many companies' technology departments: They want to protect their turf. If I am a CIO, and I don't have a data center to run and software to build, how will I be able to go to the CFO and get $100 million a year in capital expense and have 1,000 people working for me? What is my value to the company?

If CIOs want to understand their true value to a company, they need to make a total attitudinal shift. They need to ask, "How can I get the largest ROIC with the least amount of assets and the fewest number of people?" CIOs should be valued for how much business workload outside of the company's core competency they can push out into their ecosystem, not for how much they keep internally.

Procter & Gamble

Procter & Gamble has done an excellent job concentrating on its core competency. Until recently, the CIO of P&G was Filippo Passerini, and he helped the company concentrate on its core competency and develop an ecosystem of companies to handle business IT functions outside that core competency by establishing P&G's Global Business Services (GBS) unit. The GBS business unit consists of direct P&G employees and business functions as well as an ecosystem of partners that provide shared business services to P&G's global business units.

The result is that P&G's worldwide business units are designed to focus on its core competencies or what P&G calls its *core strengths*: brand building, consumer understanding, go-to-market capabilities, scale, and innovation. Meanwhile, Passerini's GBS unit and its ecosystem of partners can handle business functions and technology enablers to support those core strengths.

One of the challenges of a horizontal integration model is that it is harder to manage because the company or business unit doesn't "own" all the pieces. In the structure that Passerini has designed, the outside companies are governed by standards that were set by P&G. The result is a relationship that feels less like a client/vendor situation and more like a partnership.

I'm not the only one who thinks Passerini has done an excellent job. He is well respected in the industry. He speaks regularly to industry groups and companies, and during these speaking engagements, he discusses the role of IT and shared services at P&G. For a quantitative measure of what Passerini has built, look at P&G's ROIC. Though P&G is one of the largest corporations in the world, it has virtually no IT assets. Rather, P&G has a robust ecosystem of IT providers like Hewlett Packard Enterprise that runs its technology infrastructure, primarily on a consumption basis.

The numbers speak for themselves. P&G self-reports that P&G's Global Business Services with its ecosystem of partners has delivered $800 million in cost savings, and costs as a percentage of sales has been reduced by one-third since 2003.

Security and Continuity

Some of the resistance to cloud computing has to do with fear. One element of that fear is concern about *security*, and another element involves *business continuity* including disaster recovery. Both are certainly legitimate concerns.

Interestingly, technology security breaches of businesses have rarely involved someone accessing data in cloud environments. Security breaches more often result from lost laptops, stolen storage tapes, and other traditional theft. Network security breaches that have occurred overwhelmingly involve breaches of a company-owned IT network, not breaches of a cloud provider. Why? Because most companies' core competency is not running IT.

The core competency of a cloud provider is running a data center. Who would you expect would run a data center more securely—Hewlett Packard or Home Depot? Hewlett Packard isn't expected to sell much in the way of building supplies, so why should Home Depot be expected to run state-of-the-art computer centers? Unless running a data center is the company's core competency, that company is far less likely to be up to speed on the latest software, hardware, processes, and governance concerning security.

Some say that in today's world, security breaches are inevitable, but security breaches of enterprise cloud providers are rare. The breach of Apple's iCloud is often cited when discussing cloud security. We must remember that Apple's iCloud is a consumer cloud for non-sensitive data. That's a very different type of cloud environment than the enterprise solutions offered by providers like Hewlett Packard, Microsoft, and IBM.

Unfortunately, security breaches of corporate traditional IT is not nearly as rare. I ask many of my clients the same question "Do you and your company want to show up on the front page of the Wall Street Journal due to an IT security breach?" Keep running your own IT infrastructure and more than likely you will.

Standards

I educate executive teams about the standards that exist in cloud computing, and I tell their CIOs to look into those standards to help their enterprises become comfortable with the cloud.

The most important organization in the area of cloud security is the International Organization for Standardization (ISO). ISO is an independent nongovernmental organization, and it's the primary developer of international standards. The ISO is based in Geneva, Switzerland, with a membership of 166 countries, and it defines global standards. ISO has published more than 19,500 international standards, covering every industry from technology to food safety, from agriculture to healthcare.

An international standard is a document that provides requirements, specifications, and guidelines to ensure that materials, products, processes, and services are safe, reliable, and of high quality. For businesses, the ISO standards are strategic tools that reduce costs and increase productivity by minimizing waste and errors. Such standards help company's access new markets and also facilitate free and fair global trade.

The most important document for assessing the security of cloud computing is ISO 27002, which provides best-practice recommendations for information security management. The goal of this standard is the preservation of confidentiality, integrity, and availability. As of mid-2015, the current version of this document is ISO 27002:2013, which considers fourteen areas of security, including human resources, asset management, cryptography, physical and environmental security, operations security, and supplier relationships. Within each area, the standard specifies and outlines information security controls and their objectives. These controls are generally regarded as best practices. For each of the controls, the standard provides implementation guidance.

Each business is expected to undertake a structured information-security risk-assessment process to determine its specific requirements before selecting controls that are appropriate for its particular circumstances. This leaves the door open for users to adopt alternative controls if they wish, provided that the key control objectives relating to information security risks are satisfied. This helps keep the standard relevant, despite the evolving nature of information security threats, vulnerabilities, and trends.

In addition to ISO 27002, there are a several other important standards, including ISO 27018 (focusing on data privacy), ISO 27031 (concerning disaster recovery standards), and ISO 27036 (on the relationship between a client and a cloud provider.)

CIOs can also utilize the services of the Cloud Standards Customer Council, an advocacy group dedicated to accelerating the cloud's successful adoption and examining the standards, security, and interoperability issues surrounding the transition to the cloud. The council complements existing cloud standards efforts and establishes client-driven requirements to ensure that cloud users will enjoy the same flexibility and openness they have with traditional IT environments. The council's founding members include IBM, Kaavo, Rackspace, and Software AG.

Generally speaking, CIOs need to document and implement three types of standards for their companies:

- Advisory standards like those of the ISO
- Standards produced by other organizations, such as the Cloud Standards Customer Council
- Standard specifications that the firm uses with all the compa nies in its ecosystem

As the role of the CIO evolves from building, running, and managing operational IT to acting as a service broker who manages an ecosystem of companies whose core competencies are IT, CIOs must focus on ensuring uniform standards and governance throughout the ecosystem. These standards will include more than security standards. It will be a framework that defines the specific policies, controls, procedures, and processes within the company to ensure that all IT standards are implemented by the ecosystem. Understanding and implementing these standards is and will be their biggest responsibility going forward.

Business Continuity

Another major fear companies have about cloud computing is losing control. CEOs say to me, "If we don't own our IT infrastructure, how can we protect ourselves from catastrophic loss? What happens if twenty data centers shut down at my cloud provider?" CEOs realize that they and the company will be blamed by customers and the media. They may feel that their only recourse in such a situation would be to complain to the company handling their IT. My response to this concern is to go back again to the idea of core competency.

Every company needs a business continuity and disaster recovery plan, which should be in place whether the technology environment is owned by the company or is part of a larger ecosystem. And who is most likely to have a good, tested IT disaster recovery system? A company whose core competency is technology? Or, a company whose core competency is making widgets? No CIO should let a company into the ecosystem if it doesn't comply with the aforementioned ISO disaster recovery standards, particularly ISO 27031.

So we're back to the original thesis of this book: Every company must have a fanatical focus on its core competency. The convergence of technologies like those provided in the cloud provides companies an opportunity to bring new life to that focus and achieve the flexibility of a continual transformation environment. Focus + Flexibility = Competitive advantage. You have not started on the road to that outcome unless you are dedicated to establishing a cloud-based consumption IT infrastructure.

Who Coined the Term Cloud Computing?

Now that every technology company in America seems to be selling cloud computing, we decided to find out where it all began. The following is taken from an October 2011 *MIT Technology Review* article titled "Who Coined 'Cloud Computing'?"[1]

Cloud computing is one of the hottest buzzwords in technology. It appears 48 million times on the Internet. But amidst all the chatter, there is one question about cloud computing that has never been answered: Who said it first?

Some accounts trace the birth of the term to 2006, when large companies such as Google and Amazon began using "cloud computing" to describe the new paradigm in which people are increasingly accessing software, computer power, and files over the Web instead of on their desktops.

But *Technology Review* tracked the coinage of the term back a decade earlier, to late 1996, and to an office park outside Houston. At the time, Netscape's Web browser was the technology to be excited about and the Yankees were playing Atlanta in the World Series. Inside the offices of Compaq Computer [now Hewlett Packard Enterprise], a small group of technology executives was plotting the future of the Internet business and calling it "cloud computing."

Their vision was detailed and prescient. Not only would all business software move to the Web, but what they termed "cloud computing-enabled applications" like consumer file storage would become common. For two men in the room, a Compaq marketing executive named George Favaloro and a young technologist named Sean O'Sullivan, cloud computing would have dramatically different outcomes. For Compaq, it was the start of a $2-billion-a-year business selling servers to

---

[1] Reproduced with permission of Association of Alumni and Alumnae of the Massachusetts Institute of Technology.

Internet providers. For O'Sullivan's startup venture, it was a step toward disenchantment and insolvency.

Cloud computing still doesn't appear in the Oxford English Dictionary. But its use is spreading rapidly because it captures a historic shift in the IT industry as more computer memory, processing power, and apps are hosted in remote data centers, or the "cloud." With billions of dollars of IT spending in play, the term itself has become a disputed prize. In 2008, Dell drew outrage from programmers after attempting to win a trademark on "cloud computing." Other technology vendors, such as IBM and Oracle, have been accused of "cloud washing," or misusing the phrase to describe older product lines.

Like "Web 2.0," cloud computing has become a ubiquitous piece of jargon that many tech executives find annoying, but also hard to avoid. "I hated it, but I finally gave in," says Carl Bass, president and CEO of Autodesk, whose company unveiled a cloud-computing marketing campaign in September. "I didn't think the term helped explain anything to people who didn't already know what it is."

The U.S. government has also had trouble with the term. After the country's former IT czar, Vivek Kundra, pushed agencies to move to cheaper cloud services, procurement officials faced the question of what, exactly, counted as cloud computing. The government asked the National Institutes of Standards and Technology to come up with a definition. Its final draft, released this month, begins by cautioning that "cloud computing can and does mean different things to different people."

"The cloud is a metaphor for the Internet. It's a rebranding of the Internet," says Reuven Cohen, cofounder of Cloud Camp, a course for programmers. "That is why there is a raging debate. By virtue of being a metaphor, it's open to different interpretations." And, he adds, "it's worth money."

Part of the debate is who should get credit for inventing the idea. The notion of network-based computing dates to the 1960s, but many believe the first use of "cloud computing" in its modern context occurred on August 9, 2006, when then Google CEO Eric Schmidt introduced the term to an industry conference. "What's interesting [now] is that there is an emergent new model," Schmidt said, "I don't think people have really understood how big this opportunity really is. It starts with the premise that the data services and architecture should be on servers. We call it cloud computing—they should be in a 'cloud' somewhere."

The term began to see wider use the following year, after companies including Amazon, Microsoft, and IBM started to tout cloud-computing efforts as well. That was also when it first appeared in newspaper articles, such as a New York Times report from November 15, 2007, that carried the headline "I.B.M. to Push 'Cloud Computing,' Using Data From Afar." It described vague plans for "Internet-based supercomputing."

Sam Johnston, director of cloud and IT services at Equinix, says cloud computing took hold among techies because it described something important. "We now had a common handle for a number of trends that we had been observing, such as the consumerization and commoditization of IT," he wrote in an e-mail.

Johnston says it's never been clear who coined the term. As an editor of the Wikipedia entry for cloud computing, Johnston keeps a close eye on any attempts at misappropriation. He was first to raise alarms about Dell's trademark application, and this summer he removed a citation from Wikipedia saying a professor at Emory had coined the phrase in the late 1990s. There have been "many attempts to coopt the term, as well as various claims of invention," says Johnston.

That may explain why cloud watchers have generally disregarded or never learned of one unusually early usage—a May 1997 trademark application for "cloud computing" from a now-defunct company called NetCentric. The trademark application was for "educational services" such as "classes and seminars" and was never approved. But the use of the phrase was not coincidental. When Technology Review tracked down NetCentric's founder, O'Sullivan, he agreed to help dig up paper copies of 15-year-old business plans from NetCentric and Compaq [now Hewlett Packard Enterprise]. The documents, written in late 1996, not only extensively use the phrase "cloud computing," but also describe in accurate terms many of the ideas sweeping the Internet today.

6

The Future Is Mobile

As I walked down the street while talking on the phone, sophisticated New Yorkers gaped at the sight of someone actually moving around while making a phone call. Remember that in 1973, there weren't cordless telephones, let alone cellular phones. I made numerous calls, including one where I crossed the street while talking to a New York radio reporter— probably one of the more dangerous things I have ever done in my life.

—Martin Cooper, engineer and inventor of handheld mobile phone

Our family has always shared a passion for wine—wine tasting, having a good bottle of wine with the right meal. I think it stems from my wife's love of everything culinary. As a chef, she knows that a great bottle of wine, regardless of price, can make a meal perfect.

Over time, our passion for wine has grown, finally manifesting as the desire to have what some people call a micro vineyard (it's two acres—larger than just a hobby vineyard but not quite a full-scale commercial venture). The challenge is that we live in Texas, just north of Dallas. Texas is achieving a good reputation for wines and now ranks as the fifth-largest producer of wines in the United States. Even so, not many companies here can help with the whole value chain of a vineyard—from selecting the grapevines to planting and growing them successfully to fermenting, bottling, and aging.

So just how mobile and connected a world *are* we?

Let me tell you a little about our micro vineyard, which has become very successful through the mobile technology that connects us to companies and institutions around the world.

We started out very slowly. First, I needed some education. Of course, I know how to drink wine, and I understand the basics of winemaking. However, if we were going to invest a hefty sum in a two-acre vineyard, the data analyst in me wanted to gather every bit of information available. There are some great viticulture and enology education programs throughout the United States, but with my travel schedule, regular attendance was not an option. Our first mobile stop was the University of California Davis. UC Davis Extension has a wine making certificate program online and is 100 percent mobile optimized. I enrolled, and the education has been invaluable.

Next, we had to find a *Vitis vinifera* grapevine grafted to a root-stock that was capable of growing in the clay-based soil and climate of north Texas. Our second mobile stop was the digital edition of *Wine-Maker* magazine. Here we found suppliers in California and New York that had rootstock recommendations, with case studies, for our climate and soil type. Soon we had Cabernet Sauvignon, Sauvignon Blanc, and Chardonnay *Vitis vinifera* vines grafted to a special root-stock suitable for the north Texas soil and climate growing outside our back door.

However, growing is just the start. Every vineyard has bugs and fungi just waiting to destroy your investment. Texas A&M University has an Agrilife Viticulture and Enology Extension. Soon I had rec-ommended fungicide and insecticide spray schedules on my smart-phone, with mobile alerts to remind me to spray. If one of the vines started to appear ill, I snapped a quick photo on my smartphone and e-mailed it off to the Agrilife extension. Now I had professionals tell-ing me all about downy mildew and the use of dithane 45 and sulfur as a fungicide. All without stepping outside the vineyard.

The mobile stops in our vineyard journey continued. Mobile apps from Midwest Supplies and MoreWine Professional for supplies. Mobile apps for laboratory analysis and calculations from ETS Laboratories and Oenotools. We even did a mobile stop in Hungary, where we found a company willing to consider adding some Texas Live Oak to the traditional Hungarian Oak Barrel they produce. My wife gave me a somewhat strange look one day when she saw me using Apple FaceTime to chat with a great fellow named Bence from Hungary while sitting on a bucket in the middle of the Chardonnay vine rows.

Without meeting with a single local company, without making even one trip, we were able to share soil analysis, water analysis, and photos of the growing patterns of our grapevines with an ecosystem of providers, and we eventually chose the proper grapevines for our north Texas soil and climate.

Today Prosper Estate Vineyards (prosperestate.com) has more than three hundred vines planted on a little over an acre, with a thriving selection of Cabernet Sauvignon, Sauvignon Blanc, and Chardonnay grapes. After five years of growing, we bottled our first Cabernet Sauvignon in 2013 (see Figure 6-1), and today we produce around fifteen hundred bottles annually. That first vintage is not quite an Opus One, but I would put it up against almost any twenty-dollar California Cabernet Sauvignon any day of the week!

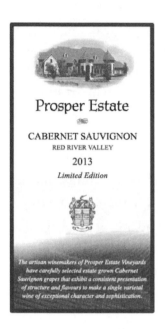

Figure 6-1 Prosper Estate Vineyards is thriving by utilizing mobile technology.

All of this happened because we were able to build an ecosystem of providers whose core competencies aligned with and facilitated the needs of our vineyard. The real beauty was that we did it all with no IT department and mostly via mobile technology. All that research was done seamlessly through cloud communities—by sharing documents, results, and real-time data—and it was all done in a utility fashion, without any bandwidth spent on the actual technology. Instead, we used the technology as a utility to achieve an outcome.

My experience is not unlike many others. We use mobile technology and apps to perform numerous and complex activities in our personal life. However, in our business lives, we seem to be frozen in time. We don't have easy to use mobile access to a myriad amount of data and functionality that would benefit us at work.

When I talk to my clients about mobility, I focus on the *consumerization of enterprise applications.* Some people refer to this as "Applification"—because the most prominent example is Apple's App

Store. Business users now expect technology enablers to be available to them anywhere (Figure 6-2), anytime, and the dynamic business environment demands it.

Figure 6-2 Apple and Google app stores provide consumption-based applications anywhere, anytime. ([bloomua] © 123RF.com)

The ubiquitous nature of mobile computing and the blending of personal and professional lives provide unique opportunities for today's businesses and their IT organizations. Not only can they improve employee satisfaction and employee productivity, they can grow market share, build customer loyalty, and increase profit margins by delivering secure, seamless, context-aware experiences in a mobile connected world. This new emerging environment provides endless possibilities—but it also brings with it some unique challenges around interoperability and security.

Traditionally, IT has focused on driving efficiencies through standardization and control. In this emerging workplace, they need to deliver applications (apps) and services in an environment where the boundaries between personal and professional life are blurred, and the enterprise may not control the entire user technology stack.

This new mobile computing environment has to address device and network security, access to applications, and privacy issues associated with having personal and company-owned data on the same device. This is true whether the device is owned by an individual or the enterprise.

IT organizations will also have to deal with changes to their financial models as they are forced to rethink their workplace models—what devices, how many, and who pays for them—and the associated support models, such as service desk or on-site support. In short, the consumerization of IT will require businesses to plan for, develop, and operationalize a comprehensive approach to enable enterprise mobility.

Most CIOs understand the need to "mobilize" their application stack. What is not as evident is the speed of change that is required. Put it this way: If your application stack is not already fully mobile enabled, you are behind.

The Mobile Explosion

I think we're all aware of the explosion of mobile phones and tablets in the marketplace. According to the United Nations, six of the seven billion people worldwide now have mobile phones. As of this writing, every sixty seconds there are 23,148 apps downloaded, 98,000 tweets posted, and more than 168 million emails sent. And more and more, the predominant method of access is through a mobile device. This explosion of employees and customers who are now untethered to traditional hard-wired communication is enabling new business models and transforming entire industries.

In the course of my work with various companies, I have noticed a dichotomy. On the one hand, CIOs understand the impact that mobility is having on their businesses. According to recent research by Xcube Labs, "Sixty-seven percent of CIOs and IT professionals believe mobility will impact their businesses as much as or more than the Internet did in the 1990s." And yet, CIOs continue to purchase and run traditional client/server software that is not mobile enabled. According to Samsung's Mobile Index Research, 24 percent of consumers surveyed currently use a smartphone or tablet as their primary work-related computing device. However, most companies' application stacks are still dependent on business users utilizing corporate-owned laptops and workstations, and many still allow access only at company-owned locations.

Gartner predicted that by 2017, half of employers will require employees to use their own devices for work. But most companies are not set up for a BYOD ("bring your own device") environment.

Here is a metric that should be a direct cause for action. In the Cisco Work Your Way Global Study, only 11 percent of end users said that they access business applications from the corporate office 100 percent of the time. This means that CIOs and IT departments are spending millions upon millions of dollars on hardware and applications that can only be used on corporate-owned hardware, mostly onsite. But only 11 percent of end users access those enablers 100 percent of the time from the corporate office? Your business users are telling you and telling the job market, "I demand geographic- and device-independent access. I demand full business technology enablers delivered via mobile devices."

As corporate IT business units become service brokers to their ecosystems of providers, they will establish architecture and standards to ensure that the IT-as-a-utility enablers they and their ecosystems provide are fully mobile enabled. The architecture and the standards it develops must be compatible with what I call a *geographic- and device-independent architecture* (GDIA). Your business users and users within your ecosystem of providers need to be able to access their technology enablers regardless of where they are located and regardless of the device they are using. To accomplish this, they must establish architecture, standards, and governance for mobile device management (MDM), service-oriented architecture (SOA), API library, mobile middleware, and security. The following sections provide a high-level overview of these areas.

Mobile Device Management

The Gartner research firm defines *mobile device management* (MDM) as "software that provides the following functions: software distribution, policy management, inventory management, security management and service management for smartphones and media tablets." Most companies have implemented basic MDM architecture and governance to allow for a minimal amount of mobile access for e-mail. However, as mobile solutions expand both within a company and throughout the partner ecosystem, more sophisticated requirements and governance will be required for application management, privacy, and auditing.

Of *great* importance is that a company's MDM program must support BYOD. A corporation should not tell employees that they have to use this cell phone or this laptop. Employees should be able to use any device they want to perform the business function for which they were hired. Individuals do not want to use one device in their personal lives and one in their professional lives. Simplicity is the new *norm de rigueur*. As Gartner predicts, whether through mandate or possibly through partial cost offset, companies will eventually ask employees to bring their own devices.

Service-Oriented Architecture and the API Library

Early in the development of its iOS apps, Apple offered developers an API (application programming interface)—a set of routines, protocols, and tools for building software applications—that they could use to design and develop apps. Thousands of freelancers created apps and loaded them onto the Apple App Store, and a whole ecosystem of new iOS software was born. As of May 2015, there were more than 1.4 million apps in the Apple Apps Store. Google followed a similar route and now there are more than 1.5 million apps in Google Play.

The business world, while behind, is following a similar path. Companies like Microsoft, Oracle, and SAP have started offering developers tools and APIs to create apps for their software. And companies have begun to adopt standards for what's called *service-oriented architecture* (SOA) for their overall IT architecture as well as mobility. If developers follow SOA standards and establish the correct architecture, any app they make should be ready to plug in and play with that company's IT footprint.

To empower mobility, an IT business unit must establish an architecture and governance model driven by an API-first approach. Mobility requires integration across numerous devices and applications. An API-first architecture will give the corporation the speed and flexibility necessary for the overall continual transformation environment. This will require a robust catalog of APIs, which aids developers—and, most importantly, the ecosystem of partners—in navigating the challenges typically associated with data storage and retrieving data from systems of record, while still adhering to authentication and security policies that can be seamlessly implemented.

The foundational purpose of SOA is to improve existing architectures by addressing the major systems as services and abstracting these services into a single domain, where they become solutions. SOA can repeatedly leverage these services in the creation of composite applications. Think of a composite application like a house. Each room can be a standalone service. However, each of the rooms are architected in a way where rooms can be combined into floors and floors into a house. SOA allows the services to be leveraged individually or, through what is known as orchestration, it can bind services together.

One important feature of SOA is the interactions between loosely coupled services—that is, services that operate independently, with as little mutual dependence as possible. Because SOA allows for service reuse, there is no need to start from scratch after making upgrades and other modifications. This enables businesses to save time and money when individual applications are modified.

SOA-built applications can be adapted quickly to business requirements as they change. It's often just a matter of re-sequencing the services invoked or reconfiguring the orchestration to modify an application.

SOA is an effective approach to many of the architectural problems businesses face when moving to a utility environment, but some IT departments see SOA as something to buy, as opposed to something to do. Many SOA projects therefore amount to purchasing technology that has been sold as "SOA in a box." You get *something* in that box, but what you get is not SOA.

While SOA has enjoyed varying degrees of success in the past, the movement to cloud and mobile computing gives it renewed value. Clouds are typically API or service driven, and are therefore service oriented. As cloud, mobility, and SaaS become absolute requirements in the IT-as-a-utility continual transformation environment operating model, enterprises must utilize SOA, which includes the use of service directories, service governance, orchestration, and other SOA-related technologies.

Mobile Middleware

Mobile middleware is simply software that connects individual mobile applications with each other and other corporate applications and systems. It is the "language" that allows apps to talk to each other and talk to the company's IT architecture.

Like other types of application middleware, mobile middleware utilizes messaging services to enable communication between different applications. The utilization of messaging services is a cornerstone of an SOA architecture and the reason why an overall SOA architecture for both mobile and non-mobile applications is so important. Other key and necessary functionality of mobile middleware includes:

- Application updates from an enterprise or public app store
- Transcoding and rendering; converting source text and multimedia assets into the correct mobile format
- Application-level security
- Messaging and notification services
- Integration brokering, including connectivity to other mobile applications and corporate systems
- Location APIs to support geo-based apps
- Capacity offload; cloud caching layer for increases in specific apps usage

Security

The importance of mobile security—that is, the security of personal and business information now stored on smartphones—cannot be overstated. Businesses and everyday users alike now use smartphones not only to communicate but also to organize their lives and store sensitive personal information. As this becomes more prevalent in the business world, new risks are beginning to emerge. Access to the sensitive information now commonly stored on smartphones must be controlled in order to protect the intellectual property of companies whose employees use them in their professional lives.

Smartphones are computers, and as such they are vulnerable to attack. Text messages, for example, can be intercepted, and sensitive information can be accessed by unauthorized parties through vulnerabilities in Wi-Fi networks or in software, from the web browser to the operating system. Unsophisticated lay users can also be tricked into downloading and opening malicious software.

Various security countermeasures have been developed for smartphones, and IT departments as service brokers should establish standards for mobile data privacy and mobile app auditing and have a partner in the CTE ecosystem able to detect mobile malware.

Mobility is at the core of the convergence of trends and capabilities that is dramatically changing the operational IT landscape for businesses. These trends are allowing companies to move to a consumption-based utility environment that embraces business-user selection of the technology enablers and business-process providers necessary to best perform their functions. The business users of today and tomorrow will undoubtedly be self-selecting mobile enabled apps.

As the IT departments of today transform into a brokerage of these IT services, they will need to establish architecture, standards, and governance that is not just mobile compatible but truly a geographic- and device-independent architecture.

City of Anaheim Develops Innovative Mobile Applications

The City of Anaheim in Southern California's Orange County is world renowned as the home to the Disneyland Resort, Anaheim Convention Center, and sports teams, including the Angels baseball and Anaheim Ducks hockey teams. But like many municipalities in today's current economic climate, Anaheim has been challenged to do more with less. In his 2012 State of the City address, Mayor Tom Tait stated that "For a variety of reasons, the city needed to cut $15 million from its budget in the last fiscal year." Although the City was able to reach a balanced budget by the next fiscal year, Mayor Tait added that it "doesn't mean our problems are solved. Our City still faces a major, long-term fiscal challenge."

Tackling these problems head-on, Anaheim turned to a visionary solution to stimulate economic development, protect public safety, and enhance quality of life. The key initiative relied on the Internet to make government more transparent and accessible to any resident or business. To achieve this, Anaheim turned to its longtime partner: HP. Together, HP and Anaheim developed two mobile applications—MyEVOC and MyAnaheim—that now make the city a leader in leveraging mobile technologies. "In our drive to reduce bureaucracy and make services easily available, we wanted to provide different modes for the public to communicate with us efficiently," says Trevor Bennett, Anaheim information systems manager. "The public/private partnership between Anaheim and HP enables us to deliver innovative, cost-efficient collaborative services to enhance public safety and quality of life."

Anaheim collaborated with HP to introduce the cutting-edge MyEVOC mobile application. MyEVOC makes essential functions of EVOC—such as police and fire incident reports, vehicle tracking and various advisories—available to city employees through smart phone devices. "MyEVOC is the next generation," Bennett says. "With EVOC, city employees can see an integrated view of city data from their desktops. With MyEVOC, they'll be able to see that data in real time on mobile devices in the field."

A pilot project introduced MyEVOC to key personnel on the city executive team. Anaheim plans soon to roll MyEVOC out to every employee with an EVOC account, some 500 of the city's 3,100 full- and part-time workers. The application was designed by HP Enterprise Services for modular scalability, so new functionality can be added as the city identifies what capabilities will be most useful. City department heads will be able to stay abreast of emergency situations while on the road, with alerts sent proactively to key personnel. Field workers such as building inspectors and utility line workers will see the latest alerts and advisories. The end result will be better decisions made faster and in close touch with developments on the ground.

While MyEVOC is for city employees, MyAnaheim is for the public at large—Anaheim's 341,000 residents, its 25 million annual visitors, and anyone who wants to download the free application to their smart phone. MyAnaheim started out with the idea of giving residents an easy way to report graffiti. When they saw the street graffiti, people could snap a cell-phone photo and send it to the city's 311 non-emergency system. The phone's global positioning system (GPS) capability was refined with help from HP to pinpoint where to send clean-up crews.

Today MyAnaheim delivers the graffiti-reporting functionality and much more, such as city events calendars; suspicious-activity reporting; utility-bill payment; alerts; and advisories. "It's a robust, bidirectional means of communication that shows the city is responsive and accountable to constituents," Bennett says. "The wide range of features makes it a highly meaningful tool—and it's available to users for free."

The benefits of mobile applications to Anaheim include better communication among city employees and with citizens; less red tape; and a more business-friendly environment for fostering economic development—all at the low cost of electronic communications. During 2011, Anaheim received 2,851 graffiti reports via cell phone, enabling quick-response cleanup of eyesores. What's more, MyAnaheim gives residents a convenient way to participate in the city's "Hi Neighbor" community outreach and awareness campaign. Whether it's addressing crime, preparing for an emergency, or putting together a neighborhood event, the Hi Neighbor initiative provides Anaheim residents with the resources they need—from events alerts to help with using social media—to get involved in their communities.

"We are all about increasing efficiencies, both internally and externally," Bennett says. "If a business owner is wondering, 'Is Anaheim a convenient place to do business?' the mobile applications reinforce that the answer is a resounding 'Yes!' The resulting economic development makes this a more vibrant community with an even stronger tax base."

Looking toward the future, Anaheim is working with HP to extend the functionality of MyAnaheim to include more disaster-preparedness features, including press releases, health care tips, emergency contacts, evacuation information—even directions to emergency pet accommodations. It's just another example, Bennett says, of how Anaheim's long-term partnership with HP enables the city to keep moving ahead. "It's not just this solution or that project—it's the entire relationship, the ability to educate me as a customer about what's possible and how to achieve it."

7

SaaS and the Enterprise App Store

*People tend to think of the web as a way to get information
or perhaps as a place to carry out ecommerce. But really, the
web is about accessing applications. Think of each website as
an application, and every single click, every single interaction
with that site, is an opportunity to be on the very latest version of that application.*

—Marc Andreessen, cofounder and general partner,
Andreessen Horowitz

Recently my wife and I were doing a little house cleaning with
our son, Henry. I have to admit that while I'm not a packrat, there are
certain things I've always just found hard to throw away. So I made a
promise to my wife to get rid of the stuff I don't necessarily need, like
my test scores from junior high school. In the attic, we came across
my very first computer: the Atari 400 Personal Computer System that
my mother and father bought me in 1980, right before I started high
school in Edmond, Oklahoma.

The Atari 400 could only be hooked up to your television via an
RF modulator, and it had a cassette tape recorder to store information
(see Figure 7-1). You could load new programs or games by insert-
ing cartridges or, in some cases, cassettes. It also had four controller
ports for joysticks and a 300-baud modem that you used to dial into
a brand-new service called CompuServe. While we loved to hear the
modem dialing and trying to connect, it rarely was successful. And

when it was successful, you had to be a rocket scientist to figure out the line command codes to use for accessing data or programs online. You couldn't actually *do* much with the Atari computer other than play games. However, you could do rudimentary word processing with the Atari Notepad program.

Figure 7-1 Atari made a major impact in the personal computer market but did not survive the inflection points of its time.

While by today's standards, the Atari 400 did not have much functionality, in 1980 I felt like I was on the cusp of something special. At minimum, I could now write my school papers on a computer. I could also store those papers on a cassette deck and then go back and edit them, and then print them on a dot matrix printer (remember *that* sound?).

Ever since I discovered *Space Invaders* at the local bowling alley, I've appreciated electronic games. Admittedly, I don't appreciate them as much now as I try to get my son Henry to stop spending so much time on video games and find something to do in the great outdoors. With the Atari I now had at home, I not only had a simple word processor, but I also could now play *Asteroids*, *Defender*, and *Space Invaders*. With every game release, the quality of the graphics improved, as did the functionality of the software that was also being released. That Atari my parents gave me was the start of a theme that has run through my entire working life: technology as an enabler.

Looking at the Atari pulled from the attic, I couldn't help thinking about the new computer I'd just bought for Henry. We've come so far in thirty-five years, from the "computer" my parents bought me that allowed me to play a few games on a black-and-white television screen. Basically, it was an electronic typewriter that could both store and edit! The new HP computer I bought Henry is called a "convertible" because it functions as both a tablet and a laptop, and when docked, it is a fully functioning desktop. It's also a phone, and a multimedia entertainment center...and it's probably more powerful than the roomful of mainframe computers that sent our first astronauts to the moon.

At the heart of Henry's HP computer is his app store. From the app store, he has ready access to what seems like an infinite amount of entertainment and technology enablers for his every need. His HP computer, combined with cloud, mobility, and the app store, is exactly the GDIA—geographic- and device-independent architecture—that we discussed earlier. Henry now has a world of data and a world of applications to meet his everyday needs as a high school senior and soon-to-be college student. No matter where he is, and regardless of what device he needs, he has it. He has Wi-Fi and 4G capabilities at his fingertips, on a device that functions as a tablet, a laptop, or a desktop. If he switches devices, tablet to phone, his app library is still available; in fact, it synchronizes to whatever device he is using. He is no longer limited by the device he's chosen or the location from which he's trying to gain access.

As important as this access without limits is, the fact that it is all available as a utility is key. No IT subject matter expertise is needed, and there are no expensive software purchases or annual software maintenance fees. Henry does not have to reach out to the mysterious IT department over and over again throughout the year for patches and upgrades. *IT is a utility for Henry and his entire generation.* When he flips the switch, his enablers turn on, and he pays only for what he consumes.

The contrast between Henry's experience and the typical business user experience of today is huge—on par with the contrast between Henry's HP and my Atari 400.

Software as a Service (SaaS)

Software as a service (SaaS) has tremendous momentum; Forrester recently projected that the market would exceed $130 billion by 2020. Historically, software has been a capital expense. A company bought software from SAP, Oracle, and Microsoft for perhaps millions of dollars and installed it on their corporate-owned IT infrastructure. In addition, the company paid annual software maintenance fees that ranged anywhere from 17 to 22 percent of the purchase price. The software maintenance agreement provided the company with patches, meaning if a client or the software company found some problem in the software, a patch would be issued, commonly for security. The agreement also gave the company periodic updates and minor releases, which added new functionality to the software. Major releases of the software package in many instances required the company to pay upfront for the software all over again. The software was installed in the company's data center, and whenever patches were required or new releases came out, the IT department had to install them as well. This could be a major endeavor, depending on how the new software integrated with the company's overall architecture and software stack and how much customization was done to the software.

For example, a company might buy human capital management (HCM) software from SAP for its HR department. A midsized company might pay $6 million for the license to install the software and another mandatory $1.2 million a year for the software maintenance fees. Then the company would hire in-house staff or a systems integrator to install and configure the software for another $4 to $5 million. The HCM software would sit in the company's data center, which would cost another $2 million in hardware purchases and $3 million annually to maintain. And every time a patch was required or an update made available by SAP, the company would bring in a systems integrator again or use its own internal resources, which would cost a few million dollars. For that HCM software, the company would minimally expend $12 million in CAPEX and lock itself into an inflexible operating model with, at minimum, another $4.2 million a year in operating expense.

Of course, that SAP HCM software might or might not have been architected or configured in such a way that it was open and compatible with other company-purchased software. So in order to get SAP's HCM software to talk to Microsoft's reporting software, more work inevitably needed to be done. For this, the IT department hired more staff or budgeted more work for a systems integrator. Just as things started to stabilize and the never-ending flow of capital expense started to ebb, the company's hardware would become obsolete, and the software company would introduce a major new release. So, the capital expense would start all over again—software licenses, hardware purchases, and large expenditures for systems integration.

This is the typical IT department. It embraces capital expenditures and a "buy, build, and run" philosophy. And as you might imagine, a lot of money changes hands during this process. In the world we now inhabit, this "buy, build, and run" model is obsolete—and the hands that used to be full are now increasingly empty. The software companies that used to be at the heart of this paradigm now find themselves in a precarious position. Business users' expectation of IT enablers has been "consumerized," and upper-level management must mandate the move to an entirely consumption-based application environment—and that means SaaS.

This is much easier to understand if you think like a consumer instead of a businessperson. When, as consumers, we want a new app for our iPhone or Android phone—a game or an app for e-mail or chat or retail payment—we go to Apple's App Store or Google Play, we download it, and we use it—without going through any IT departments. That is consumerization of the software experience, or what some have called Applification. This is normal for us as consumers; we are now very used to being able to get what we want, when we want it.

But for many of my clients, going to work in the morning means stepping out of their consumer world and back into what seems like the Dark Ages. Even today, many of my clients work in organizations that offer them and their employees no choice but to use particular prescribed computer applications for particular tasks. And these applications are still typically capital expenses requiring license payment upfront, annual software maintenance fees, and all the underlying hardware and systems integration expense required for client/server applications.

A critical factor in the success of the continual transformation environment operating model is IT as a utility. At the foundation of IT as a utility is SaaS. SaaS requires no upfront license fees, no annual software maintenance fees, no hardware capital expense or maintenance, and no expense for software patches, releases, and upgrades. Under the SaaS model, companies pay for the technology enabler on a consumption basis, and the enabler is delivered seamlessly via the cloud. A company that would once have incurred considerable capital expense and operating expense for software and hardware is now paying only a set rate per unit of consumption. Depending on the type of SaaS, that consumption fee might be user based (e.g., $5 per month per user), or it might be volume based (e.g., $500 per month per 100,000 records). There are various commercial models for payment with SaaS, but the key is that it is "metered," meaning that payment is somehow based on consumption, and expense goes up or down based on usage.

In this model, the initial software license fee disappears. There is also no annual software maintenance fee. The SaaS enabler is provided via the Internet in the cloud, so there is no need for the company to purchase hardware for that application. The application maintenance and data center costs are gone. And there are no costs for patches, upgrades, or even major releases. Patches, upgrades, and even major releases are implemented seamlessly and at no expense to the end user. Equally important, the business user bandwidth and management bandwidth spent on IT-related activities is gone, and that bandwidth can now be spent on the company's core competency and competitive advantage.

Many software companies are stubbornly holding on to the old model of license fees and annual maintenance fees. This is why they are in a precarious situation; it is a monumental business-model change for them. The big software companies like Oracle and SAP have always been able to charge large upfront license fees and mandatory annual software maintenance fees of 17 to 22 percent. Under this model, the client is responsible for installing that software on its infrastructure and incurs all of those associated capital expenditures.

In the future, with companies operating in a utility environment, large software companies like Oracle and SAP will have to adapt quickly to SaaS and SaaS payment models, or they will lose their prominence. Already we have seen independent software vendors (ISVs) relegate both Oracle and SAP to the status of second-tier players in certain software categories. SaaS providers like Salesforce.com have pushed Oracle's Siebel CRM application to second tier. Workday has pushed Oracle, SAP, and IBM to second-tier status in human capital management applications. Workday's work with Cardinal Health is an example of their success in displacing traditional human capital management software providers.

Cardinal Health and Workday

Cardinal Health is a 2014 Fortune 22 company whose mission is to help hospitals, pharmacies, and other healthcare-related businesses improve their operating efficiency. Cardinal Health's global business ranges from pharmaceutical distribution to medical supplies to clinical services. The company employs more than thirty-four thousand people.

In order to fulfill its mission, Cardinal needs to ensure that it has access to the best available talent in the industry—and Workday makes this possible. "That is the real benefit of Workday," says Patty Morrison, executive vice president for customer care shared services and chief information officer. "It helps us attract and retain the best people at Cardinal Health."

Cardinal Health selected Workday following a 2009 operational overhaul and had considered one of the traditional ERP vendors for its HR application. "[We had] heard about this thing called Software-as-a-Service," says Carole Watkins, chief human resources officer at Cardinal. "It was apparent that this was an innovative solution: the cloud functionality, the ability to have new releases twice a year, and a real customer focus."

In 2010, Cardinal Health implemented Workday Human Capital Management, and in 2015 it deployed Workday Payroll. "For us, one of the real joys of Workday is having one integrated solution," Watkins says. "It's just natural. Having one system of record and one place for employees to get information helps eliminate errors. We have implemented human capital management in most of our Asia facilities. I can remember not that long ago when our CEO would turn [to me] and say, 'Carole, how many employees do we have in X, Y, and Z? Oh, I'm sorry, you can't tell me that, right?' Now we have one place of record for things like headcount."

Workday has enabled Cardinal to attract, hire, and retain the best available talent. "In every single one of my executive committee meetings, we talk about talent. Access to information like talent cards is quick and easy, and we can look at them and say, 'What are the characteristics of this candidate, what's their background, and probably most important, what are their interests?' It's really helping us to find the right talent for the positions that are open, and, like most IT functions, we always have jobs to fill."

Workday also benefits Cardinal's employees by showing them how they can grow their careers. Morrison says, "Now Workday is helping us put discipline into the career development and planning process by using the performance management functionality. Workday builds accountability for our managers because it helps us keep it measurable."

Watkins agrees with Morrison that Workday has vastly improved the company's ability to manage talent. "Before, employees and managers would update talent profiles once a year. Now, they're living documents. They get updated every time an employee makes a move. An employee can go right into Workday and update it when they take a class, or whatever the case may be."

Morrison says that having a cloud-based HR solution has made Cardinal both more innovative and more efficient. "Cloud is a big, important strategy for us here at Cardinal. It helps us stay nimble. We're a low-margin company, so it's very important that it's very cost effective for us," she says. "And one of the reasons we looked at Workday was the speed at which we could create new capabilities for our employees and managers in the organization. Workday is intuitive, really fast to understand and to get to your information. And when you're affecting over 30,000 employees, that's really important."

Watkins agrees that one of Workday's most important features is that it provides easy access to information. "Employees are used to working on intuitive systems, whether it's shopping or online research. And it's also the ability to have information at their fingertips," she says. "Managers have quickly seen how Workday makes them more effective. When they have a question, when they need data or information, they have it at their fingertips, so they're not spending time figuring out who can get them that answer."

Workday's mobile capabilities are also valuable. "I was able to download Workday on my iPad," Watkins says. "I'll be in meetings with some of my colleagues, and we'll be talking about someone, and I'll pull the individual up. And they say, 'How did you do that? I want that. I want to be able to see their picture and remember who I'm talking about, or to find out how long they've been here, or the last time they had a career move.' So it's really proven beneficial."

Watkins says that Workday has enabled the HR organization to work more efficiently. "Workday has allowed us as HR executives to free up the thought process [in order to] focus on the things that are really going to make us successful," she says.

I've had many conversations with CIOs who say, "I would love to take my application stack to 100 percent SaaS, but the larger providers either do not have the technology or will not let me convert without a large fee." The answer to this is simple: Tell them to provide it, or you will switch to a provider that does have it. If software providers want to be a part of a company's CTE ecosystem, they must have SaaS applications with SaaS payment models. And CIOs must start putting pressure on some of the larger providers, such as Oracle and SAP, and they need to back up those conversations with movement.

A transformative CIO will say to SAP, "I'm not going to pay a $4 million a year for software maintenance fee for your accounting software. That's not where the market's going. That's not what the trend toward cloud, mobility, data, and software as a service is. We're at an inflection point, and if you, SAP, want to do business with me, put your accounting software in the cloud in a SaaS model and make it abide by the architectural and security standards I've established. I have two thousand accounts payable clerks who need software. For those two thousand users, I will give you $3 a month per user for your software as a service, which will now be part of my enterprise app store. If you can't accommodate us, I'm switching to Workday."

The large, traditional software companies haven't been eager enough or quick enough to embrace the new SaaS model because their revenue most likely will go down for a period of time, until their pay-per-usage catches up to their old CAPEX business model. New software companies like Salesforce.com and Workday *began* with the SaaS model, however. They aren't bound by the old ways of doing things. Over the next few years, companies must and will move their application stacks to SaaS models, and this must come from a CIO and C-suite mandate. Software companies that cannot embrace this transformation will lose their industry standing or disappear. In fact, I predict that several major software companies will not survive this transformation. They will either be acquired at low valuations or fade into memory.

SaaS is fundamental to IT as a utility and also to the greater thesis that companies must embrace a continual transformation environment in order to provide themselves the flexibility in the marketplace necessary to achieve competitive advantage. Who is going to have that competitive advantage—a company locked into a software package with high CAPEX and non-consumption OPEX expense and an architecture that makes change expensive and time-intensive? Or a company that can move its software platforms (and expense) up and down or left and right instantly, depending on its need?

Will SAP, Oracle, Microsoft, and IBM Survive?

You might think that large software companies are not vulnerable and have the luxury of more time to transition. Let's look at Siebel. Not long ago, one of the hottest topics in business was customer relationship management (CRM). Siebel owned the market. A large company like Hewlett Packard, with its millions of customers, needed a platform like Siebel's to manage its day-to-day customer interactions. Siebel was a traditional CAPEX software-expense operating model. It cost a set amount up front—let's use $8 million as an example—and software maintenance fees were an additional 17 to 22 percent a year (or $1.6 million in this example). That expense just gave a company *the right* to use the Siebel software, regardless of how much it used the software or what value it added. Next came the millions of dollars of hardware and IT services the company had to purchase to run Seibel. Oracle bought Siebel in 2005 for $5.8 billion, and just ten years later, it is no longer a major player in the CRM arena.

The biggest player now is Salesforce.com, which is a SaaS, pay-per-usage model. A company is billed for service based on how many people use it. There is no hardware expense. It's all in the cloud. It's all plug and play. It has security provisions that meet the ISO security standards.

Another example is human capital management (HCM). HCM applications maintain everything that an HR department needs—employee records, annual reviews, etc. The top HCM system two years ago was owned by SAP and called, naturally enough, "SAPHR." (SAP also has a system called SAPHCM, for human capital management.) Oracle, with its acquisition of JD Edwards, was also a major player in this space.

In 2006, a company called Workday entered the marketplace. Just as Salesforce.com did with Seibel, Workday is making SAP and Oracle irrelevant in HCM because it, too, is an SaaS model. It's cloud based. It's OPEX.

SaaS is here to stay, and in software, there is no such a thing as too big to fail.

The Enterprise App Store

Once a company mandates the transition of its application stack to SaaS providers, the mode of delivery to the end user is a critical success factor. Again, we must look at the consumerization of IT. Individuals have been conditioned to be able to instantly access SaaS applications via an app store. They want and expect this in their business lives as well. Companies must mandate making their application stack (which will now be in the SaaS model) available through an easy-to-use enterprise app store.

The technology to create an enterprise app store is readily available and provides a user experience very similar to that of the Apple or Google app stores (see Figure 7-2). An enterprise app store is a library of applications where individuals can choose what they want to use for their business functions. If they want to use Gmail, they go to the app store and get the app. The same is true if they want to use Apple Mail or the Microsoft Outlook app.

Figure 7-2 BMC's AppZone enterprise app store provides companies with the technology for business user self-service.

According to a recently published Gartner Research study, 25 percent of all enterprises will have an app store for managing corporate-sanctioned apps on PCs and mobile devices by 2017. This is the trend for the future, and I believe the transition will be quicker even than Gartner has predicted.

As companies move to delivering apps to their business users via enterprise app stores, we will also see BYOA—"bring your own application." Business users will provide the buying signals—and, to a degree, the testing—that determine which apps will become part of the enterprise app store. The IT department of the future will establish standards and governance that the CTE ecosystem must adhere to in order to be placed in the enterprise app store. This is its role as a service broker to the business users. However, business users will have a mechanism for recommending and even facilitating the inclusion of apps in the app store.

How Employees Pay for Apps

When SaaS and applications are provided to business users through an enterprise app store, applications and software budgets will change. Application budgets (including the necessary IT infra-structure budgets) are now primarily held by the IT department. In the future, IT budgets will utilize a distributed model. Since payment is based on consumption, and selection via the enterprise app store will be based on business user preference, budgets will be distributed to the business users' groups.

Initially companies will pay for the apps they use in several ways. Some of my clients already budget by department. They can see what apps people are using and the expense for every app. When an employee goes into the app store and establishes himself or herself as a user of Salesforce.com, a usage charge from that provider is simply billed to that employee's department.

Eventually, I believe that the charge will be made at the individual or manager of record level. Employees will be given an allowance—either X number of apps or X dollar amount worth of apps, at their discretion. For example, customer service representatives might have a restricted allotment because they don't need many applications to perform their jobs. CRM applications might be critical, but not ana-lytics or graphic design applications. A business analyst in finance, on the other hand, might have more discretion to choose from the apps available for use. The day is rapidly approaching when your manager of record will say, "Scott, you have $100 to spend monthly on the enterprise app store."

Outstanding App Stores

CIOs should examine a number of outstanding enterprise app stores as they develop their own app stores. Apple and IBM recently formed a partnership to develop an enterprise app store. Apple, which owns the largest market share of consumer apps, now wants to own the largest installed base of corporate apps, too.

With this partnership, Apple and IBM hope to bring about mobile-led business change, grounded in four core capabilities:

- A new class of more than a hundred industry-specific enterprise solutions, including native apps developed exclusively for iPhone and iPad

- Unique IBM cloud services optimized for iOS, including device management, security, analytics, and mobile integration

- New packaged offerings from IBM for device activation, supply, and management

The new IBM MobileFirst for iOS solutions draws on the distinct strengths of each company, combining IBM's Big Data and analytics capabilities with Apple's renowned consumer experience, hardware and software integration, and developer platform.

The apps created by this collaboration will transform how businesses and employees use iPhones and iPads and will enable companies to greatly improve their efficiency.

In 2009, General Electric launched an enterprise app store for its employees; it called this store GE AppCentral (no relation to the vendor of the same name). Collectively, GE's employees have downloaded more than three hundred fifty thousand applications. Users can access the store via their mobile phones or on the GE AppCentral website, says Dayan Anandappa, GE's CIO for digital media. Anandappa says that mobilization is an important part of GE's strategy—hence, GE's adoption of the enterprise app store.

Other companies with industry-leading enterprise app stores include Medco, Mitsubishi, and Johns Hopkins University. Universally, companies with enterprise app stores report a marked decrease in IT help desk contacts coupled with significant improvement in employee satisfaction. I did a consulting stint for almost two years at one particular client and was provided a laptop. It had virtually no pre-installed user applications. Instead, business users installed applications via the enterprise app store icon on the main screen. In those two years, I never had to call the IT help desk once for assistance. If I needed an application for project planning, I went to the enterprise app store and choose the project planning software I preferred. It was refreshing to be able to make my own decisions on what technology enabler I wanted to use and to have it all delivered in a self-service platform.

Apps within the enterprise app store are selected by the business users and IT department. Companies must "apply" to place their software in an enterprise app store, but first the IT group has to certify that they are in compliance with their security standards and service-oriented architecture.

Most app stores are hybrid app stores, consisting of a combination of public app stores and private applications. Google, Microsoft, Amazon, and Apple have the four primary public app stores, so the first thing a CIO should do is incorporate apps from these public app stores that already meet the company's standards. Then they should bring in products from semi-public app stores supplied by software companies such as Oracle, SAP, Salesforce.com, and Workday, which have pay-per-usage apps. Finally, they should bring in private apps that the company has either created or had developed specifically for the firm. For example, UPS has a private mobile app that helps the company deliver packages. These apps involve a bar code scan, a customer signing off on the UPS mobile device, and an automatic update from the device to the UPS warehouse system. It's a proprietary system owned by UPS, which is appropriate because UPS's core competency is logistics.

Qualcomm started its employee app store with a focus on learning apps, but the store grew quickly, and it is now the first port of call for all of Qualcomm's enterprise apps across all regions. This has benefited Qualcomm's learning and development function by enabling it to reposition itself as "the go-to team for all aspects of mobile enterprise productivity and support." Nearly all of Qualcomm's senior executives use the company's employee app store, and the company's employees frequently use their social tools to share links from it with their colleagues.

Software as a service and the enterprise app store are part of the convergence of technologies that can provide the foundation for a continual transformation environment. Combined with cloud and data, the convergence of these technologies allows a company to move operational IT to a true utility. This is a major step toward the creation of a flexible continual transformation environment that provides competitive advantage while retaining a fanatical focus on the company's core competency.

8

Big Data

There were five exabytes of information created between the dawn of civilization through 2003, but that much information is now created every two days.

—Eric Schmidt, Executive Chairman, Google

As I write this book, amazed by the amount of data that is always available to my clients and me, I can't help but think back on my education and early career.

I arrived at the College of William and Mary in 1984. While I studied philosophy and religion, my main extracurricular activity was intercollegiate debate (see Figure 8-1). I was on the national debate team, and we attended four or five debate tournaments every semester. A topic would be selected, and we would research that topic and formulate both affirmative and negative positions. Then we would travel the national debate circuit and debate that topic at Stanford and Baylor and West Point and Northwestern, and all the other major universities throughout the United States.

Figure 8-1 CEDA is the main college debate circuit.

I laugh now when I remember how we found data for our arguments. We spent countless hours in the *library*, copying pages out of books, and then cutting out and highlighting content and affixing it to index cards arranged by subject matter. We showed up at tournaments with what we called "ox-boxes"—those big lawyer briefcases—and each of us had a few of them, all filled with data about every possible aspect of that topic...both for and against.

Looking back on this, I think, *1984 can't be that long ago*.

Then I think about the start of my business career, when I worked for Montgomery Ward and Company, which at the time was the second-largest retailer in the United States. As a marketing manager, I worked on the "green screen" with a really bulky keyboard, and at the end of the week, I got a giant stack of printouts. Remember the old ledger style with the holes down the sides, green and white bars across the middle? The younger generation probably does not!

I got those sales printouts by store, by department and product line, and by SKU, but we were always working with data that was a month old. I sifted through those piles of green bar reports, trying to help the merchandisers with their go-to-market strategy and tactics. And that was just the early 90s.

After that, everything just kept speeding up. By the time I began consulting for Fortune 500 companies in the early 2000s, going to the library had become unthinkable for most people. The index cards and green bar reports were long gone. I could query an enterprise data warehouse and get sales and operations figures that were only a few days old. But this was still very structured sales and operations data. No open-ended questions were allowed; only specific questions like "What were sales in this product line yesterday?" and "What's the three-month trend line?" Of course, when I say we could ask the enterprise data warehouse a question, I really meant entering SAS code that corresponded to the question.

By 2003, clickstream, more operational data, and a wealth of marketing data started pouring in. The amount of data had exploded so much that it was more than the data warehouse could store. Much of that data had to be set aside.

Now, in 2015, I still have all my very detailed operational and sales data. I have massive amounts of clickstream and online data, supplemented with a never-ending supply of marketing data. I can now even really ask my computer via a microphone the question "What were sales in XX product line yesterday?" and the software will query the database and provide the results. But now it seems like every device and touch point in the world is sending me even more data. Welcome to the Internet of Everything and Big Data. All the partners in my ecosystem, all of my customers, my retailers and even my products are sending me data now. How do I manage this data?

The inflection point we are seeing today—and the convergence of cloud, mobility, apps, and data—is providing a tremendous opportunity. This convergence will allow us to truly harness Big Data (see Figure 8-2) to drive our business. The current dynamic business environment requires constant flexibility. Data is key to not just reacting but predicting how your business will need to change in the future compared to your competitive advantage strategy—and a continual transformation environment gives you the flexibility you need to make that change instantly. Professor Gary King, director for the Institute for Quantitative Social Science at Harvard University, once said, "Big data is not about the data." He was making the very accurate point that while data is plentiful and now easy to collect, the real value is in the analytics.

Figure 8-2 Convergence of trends allow us to not only manage but use Big Data.

We have devoted much of this book to discussing the continual transformation environment, how companies must be fanatically focused on their core competencies, and why functions and processes outside the core competency must be delegated to an ecosystem of providers. The combination of the core business and the ecosystem of providers will be powered by an operational IT-as-a-utility environment. This is the continual transformation environment that drives competitive advantage, and a company that cultivates this environment will have few if any company-owned IT assets. However...

Data: A Company's Core Asset

Data is one of those assets that a company must keep close. No matter what your core competency, your data is a core asset, and your operating model should be data-centric.

With the convergence of various technologies, including cloud, in-memory computing, and data processing applications such as Hadoop, we now can store data in a data lake, where it doesn't have to be a one-size-fits-all structure, and we can still real-time query it for business outcomes. Most importantly, access to that data is not restricted to a few data analysts. Access is allocated throughout the company to line workers, managers, and executives.

How different today's world is from those late nights we spent at the College of William and Mary library, copying data and affixing pertinent information to index cards.

Prior to the advent of data lakes, companies would build enterprise data warehouses using Oracle, or Teradata, or Microsoft SQL Server or other database management systems. The enterprise data warehouse had to have a predetermined physical structure, which required data to be placed into a field and then into a table. Then, every week or even every night, batch processing called ETL—extract, transform, and load—was undertaken. A business would take sales data from its point-of-sale register system, drive it through the ETL process, and store it in the enterprise data warehouse. It would do the same for operational data and clickstream data from its company website.

Depending on the size of the enterprise data warehouse, a business might have servers, or it might have an appliance, like Teradata or Netezza. It would also have a business intelligence application to do standard reports, or it might have a data mining application like SAS or SPSS. If the company queried the data warehouse a question, it would receive an answer to that query within a few minutes or overnight or in several months, depending on the complexity of the query. But the question always had to be structured to fit the fixed table and field structure of the database.

Every couple years, the IT department would revise and enhance the data warehouse. It would hire a company like Knightsbridge (acquired by Hewlett Packard in 2006) to do a business requirements project. Consultants like me would work with the marketing, finance, and human resources departments—and other departments, as needed—to identify their data and business intelligence requirements. Next, we would collaborate with the IT department to turn those business requirements into technical requirements. Then we would redesign the underlying data warehouse, reporting, and analytics layers. Today, in most companies' data warehouses, the designs of the tables and the fields within the tables are all based on data streams of years ago. To put it mildly, today's Big Data capability has changed things.

Big Data and the Internet of Everything

Big Data began when web browsing came into being and businesspeople started tracking consumer actions online—which websites consumers visited, when they visited, how long they spent browsing certain products or services, which messages resonated with them, and so forth. This was referred to as *click-through data*. Prior to that time, companies primarily collected customer order data and operational data. Around 2002, clickstream data blossomed and suddenly brought a huge amount of new data into corporate systems.

However, that amount of data pales in comparison to what is available for analysis now because of what we described previously as the Internet of Everything (IoE) or Internet of Things (IoT). Our machines, clothes, cars, houses, and phones are all (or will soon be) connected. For example, most 2015 automobiles are Internet enabled. Thanks to the IoE, you can use GPS to track your car's location, you can calculate your gas mileage, you can use the API on your car's computer to see whether anything is malfunctioning, and you can determine when you need an oil change.

Your home is also connected through your alarm system, which sends data that allows you to monitor your home when you are on vacation or at work. Many homes also have a heating, ventilation, and air conditioning (HVAC) system that can automatically recognize a sudden dip in temperature in part of the house and send you an e-mail alert, telling you about a broken window or some other problem. Even coffee machines are becoming Internet enabled. If you are at work, you will be able to instruct your machine at home to have a cappuccino waiting for you when you arrive. Instead of having to travel to a tiny café in Italy with a barista who knows your tastes and desires, you've brought that Italian barista home.

This scenario is here today: your car can recognize when you are ten miles from your home and ask, "Do you want me to tell the HVAC system to bring the house up to sixty-eight degrees? It has been sixty degrees all day because no one's been at home. And do you want me to tell the coffeemaker to have a cappuccino waiting for you? If so, please specify whether or not you want your milk with extra froth. According to the calendar, all the kids are at a school event, and your wife will be late getting home from work, so I've recorded ESPN News for you to get an hour of relaxation."

Your watch can now be a health monitor, tracking your heart rate, blood pressure, and blood sugar. Wireless chips can be attached to the bodies of people with diabetes to alert them that their sugar level is crashing by sending messages to their cell phones.

The amazing new world of the Internet of Everything is generating enormous amounts of data, so let's clearly define the term *Big*

Data. A generally accepted definition of Big Data from the Oxford English Dictionary is, "Extremely large data sets that may be analyzed computationally to reveal patterns, trends, and associations, especially relating to human behavior and interactions." A more functional definition of Big Data is *all data*, meaning the data from the Internet of Everything.

But how do you use Big Data to focus on your core competency? How do you use Big Data for decision making that takes advantage of your continual transformation environment in order to create a competitive advantage? I recommend taking a refreshingly cool plunge into a data lake.

Data Lakes

What is a data lake? To answer that question, here's an analogy: an enterprise data warehouse is like an ice cube tray. It has a certain structure so it can create the cubes, but it can only hold so much water, and the ice cubes it contains can look only a certain way. Similarly, in enterprise data warehouses, data was stored on hard drives within storage area networks (SANs), and when users had a query, it would be sent to those tables so the data could be brought into memory and the question answered. With today's computing power and software advances, there is no need for a predetermined data warehouse structure. A *data lake*, therefore, is a place where a vast amount of raw data can be stored in its native format until it is needed.

The term *data lake* is an accepted description for any large data pool in which the schema and data requirements are not defined until the data is queried. In addition, in a data lake, data does not have to be stored exclusively on an individual server or in a data center; it is instead stored everywhere using applications like Hadoop, and the most-used data can be stored and utilized "in memory." (Data *is* backed up on a hard drive, though, for disaster recovery.)

What does this mean for businesses? When people ask questions, they don't need data to be preconfigured a certain way. This enables them to look at the data and ask it questions in real time, with the help of map and reduce applications and data mining tools that make sense of the ever-churning data lake.

Let's use another analogy to understand this new world of Big Data. Imagine that you are an architect commissioned to design a house. First, you ask the family who hired you what their needs are and what their budget is, and then you draw up a blueprint. After they okay the blueprint, you start building the house. Once the house is built, if this family wants a new feature—a sauna, for example—you have to design an addition to the house and build it. That new design and new construction equals new expense.

In a similar way, when IT architects built a data warehouse, they tried to think of every conceivable use for the data in that warehouse and designed the warehouse for a world with a limited number of reports and queries. If a business wanted anything added on to its warehouse, the IT architects had to rebuild or add to the warehouse.

In the new world of data lakes and the cloud, there is instant expansion capability. It is as if a homeowner can close her eyes and say, "I want a new sauna," and when she opens her eyes, it magically appears. The next day, she adds a home theater. The third day, she dances in a huge ballroom made for a party that very evening. In effect, businesses now have a magic "house" where all their data is available in real time, stored in memory, with such enormous computing power available that all the company's needs can be attended to instantaneously. The beauty of the data lake is that there is no extra expense for each redesign and rebuild as each room is a virtual structure built on-the-fly and not a physical structure like the data warehouses of old.

The companies at the forefront of data lake usage are Facebook, Yahoo, eBay, GE, and Orbitz. For example, Facebook has more than 2 billion users, and all their data is coming in and being analyzed in

real time; based on that data, the company makes actionable decisions about targeting efforts and advertising. If one of your Facebook
friends "checks in" at a Starbucks, and you "like" Starbucks coffee,
suddenly an ad for Starbucks appears on your Facebook homepage.
This type of targeting would be impossible without the new model of
data storage and access. Everything's changing and adapting in real
time—to the great advantage of any company that is able to use a
data lake.

Some companies are still working on their original enterprise data
warehouses. I tell such companies to stop the madness. No company
should be spending resources on building static data warehouses and
inflexible reporting platforms. It should be analyzing information that
comes from a data lake so it can maintain its competitive edge.

It's time to go for a swim.

Who Gets and Who Doesn't Get Big Data

Let's take a look at a company that is deploying Big Data technology in some very traditional sectors. Not long ago, Amazon decided
that manufacturing diapers would be a pretty easy thing to do. Diaper
technology hasn't advanced much over the past hundred years, except
for disposable versus non-disposable. Some would say diapers are a
fairly commoditized business (or so they thought).

In December 2014, Amazon sent a wave of fear through the consumer packaged goods (CPG) industry when it announced that it was
going to manufacture and sell diapers on a subscription basis (see
Figure 8-3). Amazon can drop off a bundle of its diapers every Mon-
day, now by mail and soon by drones. And because so much data is
available to Amazon from the data lake, it can tell by a woman's shopping habits whether she is pregnant, which in turn enables Amazon to
know when to start marketing diapers to her.

Figure 8-3 Amazon's Big Data enablers are empowering yet another round of disintermediation.

Could Amazon disintermediate Kimberly-Clark and many other CPG companies right out of business by manufacturing commoditized packaged goods and using its data lake as its core competitive advantage? Are these older titans spending too much of their bandwidth gathering data in old antiquated data warehouse structures and too little analyzing it? Amazon now has to spend very little time and few resources gathering and storing data, but it spends a lot of time understanding and reacting to it.

You can begin to see how Amazon's competitive advantage will put at risk many commodity products that currently crowd the shelves of Walmart, not to mention your local supermarket: coffee, shampoo, razors, soap. Jeff Bezos clearly has a plan—as he did originally with books—to skip the wholesaler, the distributor, and the retailer and go directly to the consumer. Now he may disintermediate the manufacturer as well.

Is this a brilliant maneuver? Time will tell. What we do know is that today's consumers expect companies to know what they want, and convenience and ease of use are overwhelmingly important to consumer decision making. A mom who needs diapers for her newborn baby is delighted to have a drone drop them off on her front stoop, or to have a 3-D printer in her home to "print" a new baby bottle. This saves her a trip to the store or the arduous online process of filling out a form, painstakingly copying her credit card data, and deciphering a difficult CAPTCHA—all while her baby screams from the bassinet. Consumer understanding, speed, and convenience are paramount. Anyone who's ever ordered a book from Amazon knows that, even if you don't pay for a Prime membership, you'll probably have that book within two to three days for a physical copy. And you'll have it instantly if you have a Kindle.

Realistically, this new venture was not that easy for Amazon, which seemed to forget the power of the *brand*. A company like Procter & Gamble will tell you that its core competency is brand building. And a brand builds loyalty and thereby builds lifetime customer value. Not everything is a commodity, and brands have not become obsolete. Because Amazon forgot about the power of the brand, the diaper test was not as successful as planned. Does this mean Amazon will stop with another round of disintermediation within CPG? No. It is just analyzing more data from the data lake and will be back with more disruption.

However, the question remains: Do companies have enough data to know whether or when a major inflection point is heading their way? The retail book industry collapsed over the course of ten years, retail music over three or four years, and video stores over two or three years. Which businesses and sectors will collapse one year from now? And do you have the data to anticipate that scenario and the continual transformation environment to get ahead of it? How different would the world be if Virgin Records had invented the iPod and iTunes store? If Sears had created the first real online marketplace like Amazon? Or if Blockbuster Video had created YouTube and Netflix?

The disruptive companies of the future will have thorough under-standing of the current market environment and an ability to pre-dict future scenarios—which will all be data driven. This data-driven knowledge, coupled with a continual transformation environment to react instantly, will drive competitive advantage. These companies eschew the old paradigm, and they utilize Big Data to create a *new* system that is smarter, faster, and better. Most important: their sys-tem works.

Inside the Obama Campaign's Big Data Analytics Culture[1]

Many individuals do not know how important Big Data was to Barak Obama's presidential campaign. Several articles, some tech-nical and some strategic, have been written about the role that Big Data played in President Obama's victory. Michael Goldberg gath-ered many of those data points, which are presented here.[2]

The Obama for America campaign was about facing off against Mitt Romney for the White House. It was about the US economy, jobs, taxes, the national debt, America's standing in the world, and immigration. But behind the scenes, the Obama campaign was about creating an analytics culture so that everyone—from tens of thousands of field workers to more than a hundred data analytics experts—collected data, measured outcomes, and refined market-ing, communications, and fundraising programs to achieve results (see Figure 8-4).

---

[1] This article originally was published on Data Informed (data-informed.com). Reprinted with permission.

[2] Goldberg, Michael. "Inside the Obama Campaign's Big Data Analytics Culture," http://data-informed.com/inside-the-obama-campaigns-big-data-analytics-culture/, January 28, 2013.

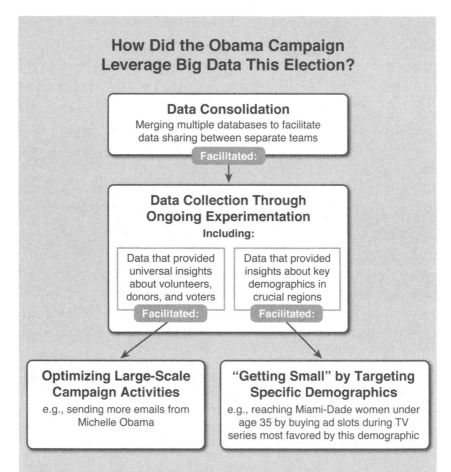

Figure 8-4 President Obama's use of Big Data has forever changed political strategy and tactics.

The demand to measure everything in the $1 billion campaign—"to put an analytics team inside [headquarters] to study us the entire time to make sure we were being smart about things"—came from campaign manager Jim Messina when he began to build the team in April 2011, said Chris Wegrzyn, a technology leader for the Obama for America analytics team. Wegrzyn said it fell to him and his colleagues to figure out how to meet this demand and to build the team and processes to do it.

"The most fundamental thing we did was to create an analysts organization within the campaign," said Wegrzyn, who is now director of data architecture at the Democratic National Committee. He was speaking during a January 24 webcast sponsored by HP Vertica.

While a lot has been written about the role data and analytics played in the 2012 race, it will still take time for political scientists, historians, and business school case-study authors to tease out all the takeaways. And for his part, Wegrzyn was not forthcoming about every detail. For example, he declined to cite specifics about algorithms his team used to target specific voter groups, signaling that the tools represent an advantage for his team in his new job.

What Wegrzyn did share was an archetypical story of an analytics-driven organization that aligned people, business processes, and technologies around a clear mission.

Advancing Analytics Ideas Developed in 2008

A presidential campaign has the luxury of focusing on one goal: getting a majority of votes on Election Day. Wegrzyn said the campaign set up five groups—the field organization along with teams for digital, communications, media relations, and finance—to focus on three activities: registration to increase the pool of eligible voters, persuasion to win support, and voter turnout.

Over the past decade, Wegrzyn said, analytics has influenced each of these activities in different ways. The 2008 campaign saw a fragmented approach, with separate databases for voter contact lists, field volunteers, e-mail campaigns, and fundraising. A field organization might report data on voters contacted and then analysts can use metrics to track progress, and some modeling to predict voter turnout. Digital activities, like web promotions or e-mail campaigns could deploy A/B testing to experiment with different approaches.

These were independent silos of activities, but the campaign still was able to assemble data from the field and use it to create predictive models to target voters based on two aspects of their anticipated behavior: whether they were likely to vote and whether they supported Barack Obama or John McCain for president.

At the start of 2011, Wegrzyn said, his team had to figure out how to inject this kind of analysis into all activities of the campaign, not just getting out the vote, but to create systems that enabled "voter-to-voter" interactions. The challenges included delivering results on an ongoing basis for an expanded set of analytics programs, using data that was widely dispersed and of varying quality. The field organization had a voter contact database. There were separate systems for donors, for online fundraising, and for e-mail campaigns. The Democratic National Committee had its own database. And the campaign had questions about whether media vendors could provide data about their audiences that the campaign sought.

"We wanted to do social media and other things better" than in 2008, Wegrzyn said. "We were doing some holistic modeling and experimentation, and trying to figure out the right way [of doing things] in terms of real, hard results. We hadn't done it before; no one had in the campaign world. But we had a little bit of experience."

Creating a Work Environment for Big Data

Wegrzyn and the Obama for America data science team had two significant assets before it started on the 2012 campaign: the trust of leadership, who saw results in 2008 and embraced analytics as central to the effort. And access to analytics talent.

Even though the campaign "paid well below market rates," Wegrzyn said, analytics professionals from a range of backgrounds, from industry and academia, applied for jobs. The goal, he said, was to "create an environment for smart people to freely pursue

their ideas." Some team members were engineers, and not everyone knew about programming SQL queries, but everyone selected
was a problem-solver and a fast learner. (Everyone who did well in
interviews also took a test to show how they approached problem
solving.)

To create a work environment for the analysts required the adoption of big data techniques, Wegrzyn said. While the campaign had
less than ten terabytes of raw data, the analysts would end up generating many times that amount in their experiments. There were
many data sets to manage, including new sources—and the pace of
the work meant they did not have time to do ETL processes. And
the campaign needed to keep pace with the analysts' ideas.

In six months of evaluations, Wegrzyn said his team chose HP
Vertica as its analytics platform after rejecting Hadoop-based systems for most use cases (high learning curve and long development
lead time) and appliances (the team needed performance before it
needed massive storage). Vertica provided a massively parallel processing database with familiar SQL queries and a path to scalability
as analysts continued to pound on the system, he said.

The resulting environment allowed analysts and engineers to use
a common platform. Users manipulated and analyzed data using
the R and Stata statistical programming languages, as well as SQL
queries and third-party analytics programs, Wegrzyn said. (Analysts also used data mining tools from KXEN.)

Two Innovative Analytics Apps

This led to what he called an unexpected innovation, a project
called AirWolf, which helped the campaign create a connection
between volunteer field workers and digital marketing efforts. By
correlating e-mail addresses with voter information, the campaign
could connect volunteers in the field with voters. The application
used SQL queries against the Vertica database, a data reporting

tool the campaign developed called Stork to send custom e-mail via Amazon's Simple E-mail Service. Analysts also could analyze results.

The effect was a more personalized politics.

"When a volunteer knocked on the door, and [the voter] said, 'I am not sure I support the president. I would like to hear about health care law.' They would enter that into contact database," Wegrzyn said. The campaign created a means for the volunteer to follow up by e-mail with the undecided voter, to send a personalized message with information about health care policies, and an invitation to discuss the issue further. "Those were brand new for the campaign and exciting for us," he said.

Another success came with an application that optimized advertising purchases. Wegrzyn said his team employed predictive models to identify target voters. They received anonymized data from media ratings companies. Combining the two datasets and then adding pricing data for various media outlets allowed the campaign to pick the best programs during which to advertise targeted messages. Analysts ran queries to explore the data to confirm the recommendations made sense.

"We were able from experiments to get a sense at the individual level of what we termed [the] *persuadability*" of certain precise voting groups, he said. Correlating these results with ratings of those groups as television audiences directed the team's attention to optimize certain media channels for advertising.

The result was a precision-targeted advertising onslaught. The campaign made twice as many cable TV advertising purchases as the Romney campaign, Wegrzyn said. The choices sought to maximize coverage of targeted voters, rather than broad demographic groups.

"White women 20 to 29 is a diverse group. It's hard to talk about that group in general. We needed to talk about individuals," Wegrzyn said, describing the campaign's approach to personalization. "We were about taking that data and looking at it more holistically. There was a lot of experimentation and really pulling all that [analytics] together."

9

The IT Department of the Future

There's a big movement to say we're not just adding services to our business and our product; we're actually trying to design an experience. You'll see that language being used. We're in the experience design business.

—Philip Kotler, author and professor of International Marketing at the Kellogg School of Management at Northwestern University

Let me take you on a very brief trip back in time.

The year was 2008—the year the New York Giants beat the New England Patriots in the Super Bowl. Toshiba announced the formal recall of its HD DVD video formatting, ending its format war with Sony's Blu-Ray Disc. Fidel Castro retired as the president of Cuba after nearly fifty years. Danica Patrick won the Indy Japan 300, becoming the first woman in history to win an Indy Car race. The critically acclaimed *Iron Man* was released, starring Robert Downey, Jr., as Tony Stark. Bill Gates stepped down as chair of Microsoft Corporation to work full time for the Bill & Melinda Gates Foundation. The US government took control of the country's two largest mortgage-financing companies, Fannie Mae and Freddie Mac. And Dmitry Medvedev appointed Vladimir Putin as Russia's prime minister.

It was the year that Washington Mutual and Lehman Brothers both declared bankruptcy, and the Dow Jones Industrial Average suffered the largest single-day point loss in its history, falling 777.68 points.

The year 2008 also saw the launch of Groupon, a website featuring discount gift certificates offered by both national and local companies. Groupon started as a local service in the Chicago area, but it soon expanded to Boston, New York, and Toronto. Within two years of its debut, Groupon had thirty-five million registered users in more than one hundred fifty markets in North America and one hundred more in other parts of the world.

In December 2010, *Forbes* and the *Wall Street Journal* reported that Groupon was "on pace to make $1 billion in sales faster than any other business, ever." In Groupon's last full fiscal year, they posted revenue of $5.1 billion.

Time will tell what becomes of Groupon—and it will likely be a very short amount of time. Things can change quickly, and the pace of change is quickening, as discussed earlier in this book. This needs to be emphasized: IT departments are out of time for the major transformation that must take place. If your IT department does not fundamentally transform itself into a service brokerage for technology enablers of business outcomes, your company's survival will be at risk. However, if your IT department is at the forefront of this shift to a continual transformation environment operating model, then great things lie ahead for your company.

The Era of the IT Department as a Service Broker Has Arrived

The IT department of the future will not own, build, and run information technology services. Instead, it will act as a service broker for a CTE ecosystem of partners that provide technology enablers to business users.

Gartner caused a big stir in 2012 with its prediction that by 2017 the CMO will spend more on IT than the CIO. Likewise, IDC predicted that "line-of-business executives" will control 40 percent of IT spending by 2016.

According to recent research from the IT services company Avanade, these predictions are coming true, and the IT manager's traditional role is vanishing, giving way to the service broker role. This is a reflection of the changing role of IT. According to the Avanade survey, 79 percent of C-level executives said that they can make better and faster technology decisions than their IT staff.

In fact, these executives said that 37 percent of all technology spending in their organizations happens without any involvement on the part of the IT department. Furthermore, 90 percent of companies said that their non-IT business departments are partially or wholly responsible for decisions involving technology.

According to Avanade, in the role of service broker, "IT staff consults with departments across the business to better understand their technology needs and objectives, then sources internal or external IT services or partners to meet these demands." This means a shift in focus for the IT department. In the continual transformation environment operating model, the IT department will not directly perform the IT services work but will have the knowledge to find that expertise and best assemble it to benefit the business.

More than 35 percent of companies' IT departments are already functioning primarily as service brokers. Avanade said that 58 percent of companies whose IT departments are structured this way plan to expand the role of IT as a service broker within the next twelve months. In addition, 68 percent of companies reported that their IT departments contribute more to the achievement of business objectives than they did three years ago.

As the IT service broker for the organization, it will be critical for the IT department of the future to provide architecture, governance, and standards for the ecosystem.

Return of the Keiretsu

A continual transformation environment operating model demands a core competency–centric company surrounded by an ecosystem of providers in a nimble, flexible, consumption-based model. This implies that a new form of what we call a "company" is emerging in the early twenty-first century. In many ways, it is a form of what the Japanese have historically called *keiretsu*. A *keiretsu* is an ecosystem of companies—each one excelling at certain things—that collectively go after a market.

Japanese companies historically were not vertically integrated like in the United States. They have always been more likely to rely on ecosystems. The challenge the Japanese had with the *keiretsu* was that they became *too* successful. For history buffs like me, a good book on the *keiretsu* is *Keiretsu: Inside the Hidden Japanese Conglomerates* by Kenichi Miyashita and David Russell.

As American companies continue to form partner ecosystems to embrace a continual transformation environment operating model to focus on their core competencies, we will need to reconsider how we view a company as a legal entity, what ownership means, what management consists of, and what we mean by "corporate structure." These ideas are all changing dramatically and quickly. On a macro level, society and the government will need to rethink what regulation means, what a monopoly is, and what constitutes anti-competitive behavior.

Governance

Your IT department will govern the ecosystem of providers in an outcome-based fashion. In this new world, IT is no longer an intermediary between the business user and the technology or business process enabler. As illustrated in Figure 9-1, the business user has direct access to the technology or even business process services via the enterprise app store, and the IT department will monitor users' access and utilization in order to manage and govern the ecosystem. For example, an employee who needs to share content with coworkers will go to the enterprise app store and open up Microsoft Share-Point, or Alfresco, or Google Apps for Work.

IT in the Role of Services Broker

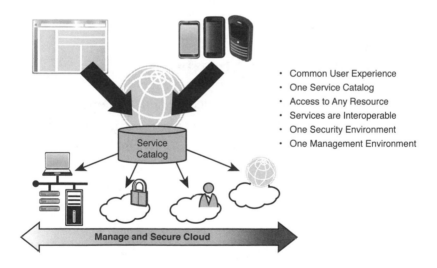

Figure 9-1 The IT Department of the Future will serve in the role of service broker.

If the IT department sees over time that all its business users are using Alfresco and no one is using Microsoft SharePoint, the department will go to Microsoft and say, "No one's using you. There's no place for you in my ecosystem because your software lacks the functionality that my business users demand." In addition, the IT department will share best practices of certain apps with business users on a regular basis. In this model, user adoption governs and drives software selection.

A smart CIO will not have to make a long-term commitment to an ecosystem of partners. Nor will he or she have to rely on one or two providers. If I were a CIO, I wouldn't bring in one cloud service provider; I'd bring in several. Never put all your eggs in one basket. Your business users are the ones who are eventually going to determine which one is best. They're accessing the services through the enterprise app store. They are the market, and the market will determine which services within the app store survive.

This is the gift of a Darwinian open market: the best services will always prevail.

IT as the Owner of Standards

As IT departments shift to a service-brokerage operating model, these departments will shrink in headcount. That is scary, I know. We are going through a fundamental transference of business roles. Technology "developers" will switch from working for end-user companies to working for companies in the partner ecosystem. IT departments will no longer own, build, and run IT data centers, hardware, and software. However, the people who remain will have a critical role in establishing architectural, security, and data standards. The IT department will say, "This is our architecture, and these are our standards. If you want to do business with us, here are the standards that you must abide by."

The IT department will thus need enterprise architects and individuals knowledgeable about SOA and governance, security standards, master data management, and partner management. It won't need application programmers and technologists to watch and fix hardware or build and run software. Currently, those jobs make up as much as 80 percent of current IT departments, so this is a seismic shift.

This is also a major shift in career planning for those entering the technology field. Companies will have fewer and fewer IT employees, and those who remain will have expertise in architecture, standards, and governance—in particular, partner ecosystem governance. We will see a massive shift as "build and run" technologists such as programmers, systems administrators, and database administrators move from client-side jobs to the SaaS and cloud provider ecosystem. In many ways, the SaaS companies and cloud providers are everyone's data center in the future.

IT Services Will Continue to Transform into Business Process Services

Just as the CIO's role is shifting, so is the place where technology ends and business outcomes and business process services begin. SaaS used to be simply applications that a company could "rent" and pay for based on consumption. They could be hosted, or they could be in the cloud. Nowadays, *SaaS* and *cloud* are fairly synonymous, especially in the consumer world. Already it is hard to tell where cloud ends and SaaS begins. And that is the way it should be in a utility environment. When we discuss SaaS, we assume that it is cloud delivered.

We are on the cusp of yet another transformation. Today's SaaS providers are starting to look more like business process as a service (BPaaS) providers. In the future, it will be difficult in some areas to see the distinction between cloud, SaaS, and BPaaS providers.

Soon the enterprise app store may do more than just connect accounting with the collections application/technology enabler of its choice. It may connect accounting with an end-to-end business service provider for accounts receivable collections.

Key to this shift is that the consumption-based payment model will remain. It will be pay-per-usage but based entirely on a business outcome. The BPaaS provider will simply charge you $5,000 a month to collect $5 million a month in receivables, with no more than ten days of sales outstanding—guaranteed. Within the CTE partner eco-system, the IT department of the future will be managing many SaaS providers, as shown in Figure 9-2. However, it will also need to gear up to manage many BPaaS providers.

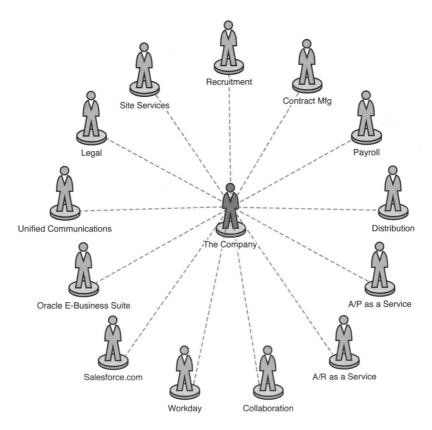

Figure 9-2 The company of the future is core competency centric surrounded by a CTE partner eco-system.

The entire CTE ecosystem of partners will move closer and closer to a business-process outcome over the next decade, and the CIO as a service broker will be prepared for this shift. Business-process outsourcing is not new—it's been around for many decades—but process and technical limitations have prevented a full embrace of much business-process outsourcing. How can your company outsource accounts receivable if you use SAP for accounts receivable, and that SAP platform sits in your data center and is only licensed for your employees to use? Under the new model, all the technology is in the cloud as a service. Why not just add the accounts receivable clerks as well and have a full outcome-based solution?

The IT Department of One

Although some futurists have written about the "IT department of one," I believe that is an extreme view of the future. There are always going to be small pieces of IT that a company should own that should not be moved out of their corporate-owned base. Of course, a company owns its governance and standards, but it should probably own the data as well. And CIOs should be cautious with payment, healthcare, and other personal identifiable information (PII) data. However, the presumption should always be that the company doesn't want to purchase any hardware or software unless it is absolutely proven that it cannot be accomplished within the company's CTE partner ecosystem.

So, as you can see, the IT department of the future is still doing a lot as a service broker, though IT departments in general will definitely shrink. In the future, IT departments will be as much as 10 to 20 percent of their current size because they will not be building or running anything.

Startups, spinoffs and Internet-based industries understand the implications and benefits of the new style of IT model better than older companies do. These industries are young—in many cases five to ten years old—and they are not impeded by old organizational, financial, and technical structures. In addition, they don't have the attitudinal inherency that may come with these old structures. The older the company, the further behind it seems to be, in part because these companies are not receiving the mandate for action from the top.

In most new company models, everybody on the payroll better have something directly to do with the company's core competency. Anyone who doesn't shouldn't be on the payroll. Which companies aren't "getting it" can be determined by looking at their balance sheets—specifically at their return on invested capital (ROIC): if they're holding a lot of IT assets on their books, they don't get it.

Ultimately, the future mode of operation under the continual transformation environment operating model demands that we also rethink the reporting structure of the IT department. A good argument can be made that only business units directly impacting and utilizing a company's core competency should report directly to the CEO. Currently, IT is part of the C-level suite, with the CIO usually reporting to the CEO. The CIO has as much authority as the CMO, the CFO, etc.

In the new style of IT as a utility, CIOs may no longer need to be members of the C-suite. They should be reporting either to the COO or to the CFO. (In the late 1970s and 1980s, that was, in fact, the chain of command.) When companies started moving away from their core competencies and became so enamored with owning and growing all aspects of business processes within the value chain, CIOs jumped up to the C-suite. That level of inclusion may still be appropriate in companies where technology is a core competency, but for most others, it's time to remodel and reshuffle some key positions. And that may mean that the CIO no longer reports to the CEO.

In fact, the farther in the background (from a business user perspective) IT and the CIO are, the better they are likely to be performing their roles. If I were a CIO, I would want to be rated by how few business users knew my managers' names or mine.

Transforming Seadrill

Terence Ngai of Hewlett Packard published a fantastic transformation story on Enterprise CIO Forum in April of 2014. He recounted the story of what he called "Mission Impossible." HP was to migrate the head office and data center of the world's largest offshore oil and gas drilling company from a traditional environment to a completely cloud-based operation for all corporate systems, relocate the executive team's systems to London, and move the corporate back office and IT to Dubai. And, the entire transformation had to be completed in only six months, at a competitive cost.

Six months. Are you kidding?

HP Enterprise Cloud Services did all this and more, successfully transforming the entire IT infrastructure of Seadrill from legacy systems to infrastructure as a service (IaaS) within a virtual private cloud.

With a market capitalization of $20 billion and offices across the globe, Seadrill requires an agile and reliable IT infrastructure that can support its business 24/7. According to Seadrill vice president and CIO Richard du Plessis, "virtual cloud gives the company the ability to react to capacity changes as demand shifts, a key benefit for business operations."

Shift from CAPEX to OPEX

What drove the move to virtual private cloud? Either the existing Seadrill data center in Stavanger, Norway needed to be refreshed, or Seadrill could use this opportunity to move to a new, better operating model that allowed it to concentrate on its core competency. The infrastructure had to accommodate the changing workload generated by company mergers and acquisitions but still incorporate legacy data center applications. Moving the entire IT application stack to a virtual private cloud keeps IT current and provides the flexibility to manage the capacity. It also shifts operations from a CAPEX model to an OPEX model, allowing the company to pay for only the resources it needs when it needs them.

By enlisting executive sponsorship from the beginning and ensuring the proper skill sets and processes were in place prior to the cloud launch, Seadrill avoided the typical roadblocks that can derail a cloud transformation. HP Enterprise Cloud Services for Virtual Private Cloud mapped out a strategy in advance to ensure that Seadrill could migrate its applications with minimal impact on day-to-day operations.

High Availability and Disaster Recovery for Continuous Operation

"The need for our system to be up and running is absolutely paramount," Seadrill VP and CIO du Plessis emphasized. A virtual private cloud gives Seadrill the assurance of high availability. Added du Plessis, "If I want more capacity tomorrow morning, I just turn the button and I get it. The more you can put into the virtual environment, the more high availability you have."

Seadrill also benefits from a "hardened" environment that guards against attacks and viruses, and helps protect against outages and data loss. Like many fast-growing companies, Seadrill had neglected its disaster recovery efforts. The HP solution provides a two-tier disaster-recovery solution that combines tape-based recovery with cloud continuity.

The Flexibility to Scale

The virtual private cloud enables Seadrill to change its data center capacity at will. There's no longer any need to consider issues such as air conditioning or other physical requirements. du Plessis states, "I can just go online and say, give me some more. To me it's like I just took a problem away, so I can focus on the things that really count for the business." The result was a virtual private cloud environment that allowed Seadrill to:

- Reduce the total cost of ownership
- Pay only for the usage it consumes
- Rapidly provision additional IT resources
- Achieve increased reliability and security
- Accommodate legacy applications

Today I'm happy to report that Seadrill is running more efficiently—and profitably—than ever before. The company made a fundamental shift in its beliefs about how it needed to deploy resources to streamline the company's core competency. Seadrill's leadership recognized that their continued success requires them to stay focused on oil and gas drilling and let Hewlett Packard worry about the operational IT. By reconstituting their approach and rechanneling company funds accordingly, they were able to get Seadrill to concentrate on the work that really matters for the business.

Seadrill's transformation speaks to the importance of making significant attitudinal and structural shifts. You might think you need to "revamp" your IT by investing in new software and hardware and a shiny new data center. But unless your company's core competency is IT, the better solution is for you to get rid of all of it.

10

Where Do We Go from Here?

Good business leaders create a vision, articulate the vision, passionately own the vision, and relentlessly drive it to completion.

—Jack Welch, former CEO, General Electric

I've always loved the Nike trademark "Just Do It." It instantly invokes the positioning of the Nike brand. It is also a much-needed lesson in management. There is time for discussion, there is a time for consensus, and there is a time when you need to "Just Do It."

My father, Jack Stawski, taught me much about business. He was the epitome of a role model, the son of a Polish immigrant who worked his way up from the plant floor to the executive suite at AlliedSignal, which was an aerospace, automotive, and engineering company created in the 1985 merger of Allied Corp. and Signal Companies.

Aside from the work ethic both he and my mom, Sharon, always showed, my father often provided me with the opportunity to observe great real-life management decision making in action. The following is one of the "Just Do It" stories that helped to shape my identity.

It was the coldest day of the year in March 1993 in Asheville, North Carolina. Most of the roads in the city were closed due to the extremely heavy snowfall. The roads were so bad that even emergency vehicles could not respond to calls. Ambulances were stranded in snow up to their hoods and could not move.

At that time, my father was the director of Materials for ITT Teves Automotive, the manufacturer of the newly developed antilock braking system for many of the major automotive producers. Chrysler, one of the company's major customers, had announced the launch of its new K Car platform, which included Plymouth, Dodge, and Chrysler. After the initial launch of this new series, sales at Chrysler took off better than anyone had expected. Consumer demand for the new platform was sensational.

Since ITT Teves was the sole source for the new ABS feature, and the Ashville plant production was at full capacity, the plant was on a 24/7 schedule. Daily production was being expedited by Chrysler and air-shipped to assembly plants. Additional capital investment for capacity had been requested from the corporate headquarters, but it would take at least a year for it to become available.

Due to the extreme blizzard in Ashville, my father was not able to leave our home. Our driveway sat on a twenty-eight-degree incline, and the snow was at shoulder level as you came down the drive to the street.

The third-shift personnel were unable to get out of the plant, so the plant became their temporary home; they ate and slept there. Needless to say, the first-shift personnel were unable to get into the plant, as the roads were closed to all traffic.

Due to the uncanny circumstances created by the weather, Chrysler was advised that ITT could not make any shipments to the assembly plants in Michigan. Chrysler's senior management immediately got involved and made it very clear that if ITT (and therefore my father) did not maintain shipments to the plants, ITT would be held liable for the plants' shutdown, and the damages incurred would be in excess of $100,000 per day for each day the plant was shut down!

What do you do in a situation like this? Management can't control the weather, after all. Well, my father was not one to let a little thing like the worst snowstorm of the decade stand in his way. He convinced Chrysler to have chartered jets on the ground at the airport in

Greenville, South Carolina, to shuttle product to the assembly plants. Now he just needed to get the product over the mountains from Asheville to Greenville.

Since he was working out of the home (thankfully we still had telephone service), he was able to communicate with both the plant and Chrysler. He knew he needed to get the roads cleared in order to have any chance of meeting Chrysler's needs. He tried the local departments responsible for clearing the roads but was unable to get them to prioritize the roads to the plant; emergency vehicles were their priority. He then contacted the local airport, looking for anyone who might know someone who could help.

Fortunately, an airport agent told him that one of local pilots had just left the airport for a convenience store to get some food and milk for his family, and the agent had noticed that the pilot had a tractor on a trailer behind his pickup. He didn't know if the pilot would be able to help, but it was a possibility. He provided the pilot's telephone number.

My father immediately contacted the pilot, and after introducing himself, told him of the problem and asked if he would be willing to plow the road and the plant parking lot. The pilot said he was not in a position to do this, as his family needed his support. After several minutes of discussion, my father asked the pilot if he would sell ITT his tractor. Needless to say, the pilot was somewhat taken aback by this question. He understandably questioned the seriousness of the offer, and my father assured him that this was not an ideal situation, but it was a serious offer. After some negotiation, my father purchased the pilot's Kubota tractor for $5,000.

He then made the appropriate arrangements for his plant controller to wire the funds directly to the pilot's bank account. Once he'd confirmed that the funds were available, the pilot agreed to drive the tractor to a mutually agreeable spot, where one of the ITT employees would pick it up and proceed to the plant to plow the incoming road and parking lot.

Although the plant parking lot and the road were now clear, my father knew that the roads over the mountain from Asheville to Greenville would still be impassable. So he concluded that the best approach would be to charter any available helicopters from Greenville and other surrounding airports and have them land in the ITT parking lot. His employees would then load the ABS units onto the helicopters and shuttle them over the mountains to Greenville, where the products would be transferred to the jets for their final journeys to Chrysler's assembly plants.

The plan was solid, except for one issue. The downdraft from the helicopters' rotors caused the snow and ice on the parking lot to freeze to their struts. After an excellent brainstorming session, the team determined that the best solution was to place wooden skids on the ground in the parking lot and have helicopters land on the skids. The solution worked, and ITT's ABS products were loaded and shuttled to Greensville on a daily basis for three days, as seen in Figure 10-1. Our neighbors told me later that the helicopters taking off and landing at our plant reminded them of a military operation.

Figure 10-1 Daily shuttle of ABS products from Ashville to Greenville. ([Bogdan Ionescu] © 123RF.com)

The success of this operation depended on clear communications, perseverance, teamwork, and the employees' commitment to the customer. Chrysler later recognized the entire plant for its efforts to overcome a major catastrophe.

The lesson I learned from this story is that sometimes you do not accept "No." You do not accept "It can't be done"; you "Just Do It."

I hope by now I have convinced you that there is value in having a fanatical focus on your core competency; that business and technology activities outside your core competency should be moved into an ecosystem of partners that provide these services; and that if you follow these guidelines, you will have the management bandwidth and operational model to continually transform your company and maintain a clear competitive advantage.

What will your future mode of operation look like once your company has made the transition and is now fanatically focused on its core competency? You have an ecosystem of partners designed around consumption-based support that doesn't incur a long-term capital expense or require an inflexible infrastructure that can't react to the marketplace. The IT department does not own its equipment anymore—no computers, workstations, servers, or software. Rather, the ecosystem of partners provides the necessary technology enablers on a consumption-based schedule. If a laptop is needed, a provider supplies one for X dollars a month. Your company no longer owns any data centers. If you need data center capacity, it's on a usage basis in the cloud, much like your utilities at home.

The software is provided by an enterprise app store. So a new employee can go to the app store and pick the e-mail program of his or her choice, without any IT intervention, and access that e-mail. The same is true for collaboration apps or sales and marketing technology enablers. All of these programs are accessed through the enterprise app store, without any IT intervention. And all of that is just consumption-based operating expense.

Once your company is fanatically focused on its core competency, and you have a continual transformation environment operating model that not only allows for change but actually *encourages* it, what can you accomplish? You can enter and exit markets at will. You can move products and services in and out of channels—this product through distributors, this one directly to retail, this one directly to consumers. You can divest and acquire at will. Your time to market is instantaneous. The question is no longer what can't you do; it is a scenario of infinite possibilities. You have achieved competitive advantage.

You now know what the future mode of operation can look like. Now, how do you get there?

Mandate from the Top

Moving to this new IT-as-a-utility, service-brokerage approach is a difficult transformation for some CIOs. They think, What will I be doing if I am not owning, building, and running all aspects of my IT department? Will I be obsolete? Will there still be a place for me in executive management? Resisting change is very human. That is why the transformation needs to be mandated from the top by those who have a vision—those who understand inflection points and trends and know how to get ahead of them.

Over the years, there has been a drive to manage by consensus and to push strategic decision making down too many levels. When you look at the actions of visionaries like Bill Gates, Steve Jobs, Jeff Bezos, and Mark Zuckerberg, it is obvious that they believed that achieving a vision requires clear mandates. These are four individuals who have at different times been beloved and unpopular with their employees. Why? Because they know that consensus management is not always the best approach. Sometimes you must mandate change and action. Sometimes, you "Just Do It."

In my opinion, companies have gone too far down the road of management by consensus. Of course, executives want line managers and employees to understand how to get in front of an inflection point and how to make the right decisions. However, an inflection point by its very nature poses a serious risk to the survival of a company and therefore has to be tackled from the top, with clear mandates.

To implement a continual transformation environment operating model powered by an IT-as-a-utility foundation, the C-suite must mandate action. A CEO needs to tell his or her company, "I don't want an RFP, I don't want business analysis, and I don't want to spend the next nine months determining alternatives." The CEO needs to tell the CIO and the technology department, "Within twelve months I want our data centers shut down. I want our entire application stack moved to the cloud. Within eighteen months, I want our entire application stack on a consumption-based SaaS model. Within twenty-four months, I want our technology enablers to be readily accessible through an enterprise app store, and I want my IT department fully transitioned so that it is a service broker to an ecosystem of providers. I want a future mode of operation that will have no operating technology CAPEX and IT headcount that is substantially reduced."

This is the objective of our era, the manifesto of successful companies everywhere. Once the CEO puts such a mandate in place, everyone in the company will benefit from the company's ability not only to survive but to thrive.

Many CIOs hesitate to take such drastic action. Frankly, they may have job security issues, and they may fear that the transition will be painful. And they may be concerned that they are transitioning themselves right out of a job. This is the wrong attitude. A very early mentor of mine once told me that you should never be afraid to recommend oneself out of a job. The minute you are afraid to make a recommendation that may mean losing your position, you start making bad decisions. Right decisions, not protectionism, ensure job security.

Three Camps of CIOs

The IT empires that have been built over the past thirty years are like all other empires—sometimes they crumble when they resist change. As I travel the country, I see CIOs divided into three camps: those who recognize the new realities and resist them; those who recognize the new realities and look for half measures; and those who recognize the new realities and are moving rapidly to a new model of IT.

Camp number one is the *traditionalist* CIOs, who often grumble and appear to want change. They say to me, "I don't like buying hardware. I don't like buying software. I don't like having to spend a large percentage of my budget every year on constantly upgrading and revising software." Then they pause and continue: "But our technology is so important to us, we don't trust anyone else to host our software or manage our software or build our software. Our business processes are unique to our company, so we can't just use off-the-shelf technology, even slightly modified. We have to be in the technology software development business ourselves. We have to build and run."

In camp number two are *incrementalist* CIOs. They recognize that things are changing and that there are developments and trends in the marketplace that could allow them to get out of the build-and-run business. They also know about the cloud and SaaS, and they have thought about transitioning a percentage of their budgets (typically a minority percentage) toward an ecosystem of partners to host and maintain the technology. However, these CIOs are moving very slowly, very incrementally. They cherry-pick the low-hanging fruit. Every few years they convert a traditional license/maintenance client/server platform to a SaaS platform, or they move some storage to a cloud environment. But they are increasingly late to the party, and they are preventing their business users from adopting the continual transformation environment operating model that can survive the massive disruption that today's inflection points are creating.

These CIOs are more dangerous to the health of companies than traditionalists because they have convinced themselves, their CEOs, and their CFOs that they are in front of a trend when they are in fact reacting to it. They are always one step behind. But they have created some movement, which others in the company may mistake for forward progress. When I talk with them, they say, "I've already taken 10 percent of my workload to the cloud. Look, I'm using Microsoft Office 365 now, and I have e-mail in the cloud!" Meanwhile, they are spending millions of dollars refreshing hardware and millions of dollars on client/server, license based, and annual-maintenance-based software that prevents the organization from achieving true flexibility.

These incrementalist CIOs haven't fundamentally transformed themselves from a build-and-run operating model. They've only scraped the surface. They are using those little scrapings to convince their management and their users that they are ahead of the new technology. These CIOs are particularly dangerous because they might give the perception of change. However, they are not really making the transformative changes that will keep their companies ahead of their competition. They're actually only maintaining the status quo, at best.

In camp number three are, of course, my favorite CIOs—the *transformative* CIOs. They recognize that they are living in a time where it is dangerous to be a traditionalist *or* an incrementalist. They recognize that this inflection point gives them a unique opportunity to totally change the IT model within the company and provide a foundation for the continual transformation operating model. They also realize that this change in their IT model will allow the company to maintain complete focus on its core competency and its strategies for competitive advantage. The transformative CIO is throwing out every preconceived notion the company has about IT and rebuilding as if the company were a startup.

Transformative CIOs say to themselves, "If I just started the company now, would I build data centers? Of course not. I'd have all my applications running in the cloud. Would I buy or build all this software? No, I would have an ecosystem of partners, and I would only pay for the software as a service. And much of it would be open source, and would fit into the architecture, standards, and governance that I have defined for my ecosystem. Now I have become a broker of IT services that meet my business-user needs rather than a developer and builder of IT services. I have the cloud to make this work. I have mobility. I have data. And I have an app store, all converged into an operational IT as a utility model. I have become the IT department of the future." That is a transformative CIO.

Attitudes and Structures

In my experience, the resistance of traditional and incremental CIOs is both attitudinal and structural. The attitudinal resistance rests on CIOs' belief that the value they add is the company-owned technology. They want to ensure that their infrastructure is always running the best it can, that it is secure as possible, and that they are meeting the needs of business users. In order to do that, they *believe* they need to own and control the technology. It is a misplaced belief.

There is also a structural challenge that inhibits change: the way companies account for their capital expenses. When an IT department goes to the CFO and asks for $50 million of capital expense to buy hardware and software equipment, that money doesn't come out of this year's profit. It is depreciated on a schedule—usually anywhere from five to twenty years. When companies report their earnings, it's EBITDA (earnings before interest, taxes, depreciation, and amortization). EBITDA makes it seem like only a small amount of that $50 million in capital actually left the bank, when it really is gone in its entirety. This gives companies a structural incentive to spend large amounts of capital because doing so has a small impact on EBITDA, which is a metric many investors review. However, the reality is that the expense has a much larger impact on the company's balance sheet, operating capital, and total shareholder return.

Under the continual transformation environment operating model, a company is going to take some hits when it moves from capital expenses to operational expenses. This is why CEOs need to explain what they are doing in terms of cash flow, return on invested capital, and total shareholder return. As a stockholder, do you want a company to spend $50 million a year in capital expenditures on software and hardware that locks it into an inflexible operating environment? Or would you rather the company write a check based on the consumption expenditures for IT of $100,000 a month, a sum that varies depending on how often business users use that software and hardware?

Most investors want the company to keep the $50 million in the bank, where it can collect interest or be put toward R&D, acquisitions, or dividends. Cash is an asset. Capital expense for non-core-competency activities is not.

CIOs as Heroes

How do you become a transformational CIO? A change in attitude is vital. Like Clark Kent, who changes from a mild-mannered reporter into Superman by putting on a different outfit, CIOs need to think of themselves as secret superheroes. If you want to make an impact on your company, go to your CEO, your CFO, your CMO, and the executive leadership team and convince them that your company needs to refocus on core competency and on creating an environment of continual transformation.

Next, you need to paint a picture of this new world. Say you have two thousand full-time-equivalent employees (FTEs) in your IT department; you are spending $800 million on IT out of $20 billion in revenue, and you have a capital expense budget of $50 million a year to buy hardware and software. You go to your executive leadership team and tell them you are going to reduce capital expenditure from $50 million a year to $1 million a year, giving them $49 million back to invest in R&D and whatever else they need. Tell them you are going to eliminate fifteen hundred of your two thousand FTEs; you only need an IT department of five hundred because you are no longer building and running anything. Rather, you are governing and setting up standards for an ecosystem of providers.

That's the kind of game-changing conversation today's CIOs need to be having with the C-suite. And it will in fact change the game your company is playing. Remind the leadership team that you are not taking IT enablers away from the accounting department, finance department, human resources department, marketing, sales, or field-service organization. In fact, you are giving them better technology enablers for which you are only paying based on usage, which will afford them flexibility where they need it without burdening them with a fixed infrastructure cost.

If you make a presentation like this, filled with financial specifics and passion, then you will not be a renegade or a pariah; you will be a hero who transforms your company in dramatic and powerful ways.

You can always avoid the issue or take miniscule baby steps. But if you do, I can guarantee that you will be joining E. F. Hutton, RCA, Eastern Airlines, WorldCom, Circuit City, RadioShack, Blockbuster, General Foods, and many other companies that at one time were at the top of their game and are either no longer in business or a shell of their former selves. These companies didn't have the courage to change. They also did not possess a roadmap for successful transformation—and even if they had, they certainly weren't ready for the ride.

You are not of their ilk. You *do* have a roadmap. And you have an executive mandate. You are going to refocus your firm on its core competency. You are going to move your non-core-competency functions and processes (including operational IT) to an ecosystem of providers. This ecosystem will provide you the foundation for a continual transformation operating model. This focused consumption-based, flexible, and proactive company will have competitive advantage.

You've witnessed both the successes of today's most adaptable companies and the failures that occurred when companies resisted change. The choice is up to you. Will you adapt to survive? Will you lead the charge to focus on your core competency and establish an ecosystem of partners to handle all the rest? Will you embrace change and transform your company accordingly?

I wish you nothing but blue skies and smooth sailing on the journey.

Think Your Company Is Immune to Failure?

Consider Circuit City, which filed for bankruptcy in 2008 and liquidated its last remaining American retail store in 2009, after sixty years in business. At the time of its demise, Circuit City was the second-largest electronics retailer in the United States (after Best Buy), with nearly six hundred stores nationwide. Through much of the 1990s, Circuit City was one of America's favorite places to shop for new electronic devices—TVs, computers, stereo equipment, mobile phones, etc. In fact, at the time, many flattering case studies were written about Circuit City as the role model of the super-sized specialty store.

As the popularity of online shopping grew, however, the company's fortunes began to sink. Circuit City had invested heavily in things that it considered to be necessary operating expenses: distribution, real estate, information technology platforms, and other large expenditures that locked the company into an inflexible operating model. While the company certainly made a number of questionable business decisions (such as abandoning its booming appliance-sales business and entering into an exclusive mobile phone sales partnership with Verizon), the real reason for Circuit City's bankruptcy may have been its inability to transform itself or adapt to changing times because it had locked itself into a CAPEX heavy business operating model.

Bibliography

Chapter 1

"2013 State of the CIO," *CIO Magazine*, http://www.cio.com/article/2369307/cio-role/79671-The-State-of-the-CIO-2013.html, Janurary 2, 2013.

Grove, Andrew S., *Only the Paranoid Survive: How to Exploit the Crisis Points That Challenge Every Company*. New York: Crown Business, 1999.

Grove, Andrew S., *Swimming Across: A Memoir*. New York: Hachette Book Group, 2001.

Lafley, A. G., *Playing to Win: How Strategy Really Works*. Boston: Harvard Business Review Press, 2013.

"Taming the Digital Dragon: The 2014 CIO Agenda," *Gartner*, https://www.gartner.com/imagesrv/cio/pdf/cio_agenda_insights2014.pdf, 2014.

Zhu, Pearl, "IT Spending Benchmark Debate: Ideally what should be percentage of IT spent of an organization relative to its revenue?" *Future of CIO*. http://futureofcio.blogspot.com/2012/12/it-spending-benchmark-debate-ideally.html. December 28, 2012.

Chapter 2

Barrie, Joshua, "Here's How the Internet of Things Will Solve Traffic Jams and Take the Stress Out of Finding a Parking Space," *Business Insider*, http://www.businessinsider.com/ofcom-report-on-internet-of-things-2015-1, January 27, 2015.

"Brand Protection through the Cloud," Hewlett Packard, Case Study, http://www8.hp.com/h20195/V2/GetPDF.aspx/4AA4-6171ENUS.pdf, 2013.

Davenport, Karen, "How Internet of Things Will Change Industry," http://www.industrial-ip.org/en/industrial-ip/internet-of-things/how-the-internet-of-everything-will-transform-industries, June 2013.

Dorf, David, "How the Internet of Things Will Shake Up Retail in 2015," *Forbes*, http://www.forbes.com/sites/oracle/2015/01/09/how-the-internet-of-things-will-shake-up-retail-in-2015/, January 9, 2015.

Dougherty, Paul, Prith Banerjee, and Alan Alter, "5 Ways Product Design Needs to Evolve for the Internet of Things," *Harvard Business Review*, https://hbr.org/2014/11/5-ways-product-design-needs-to-evolve-for-the-internet-of-things, November 5, 2014.

Evans, Dave, "The Internet of Things: How the Next Evolution of the Internet Is Changing Everything," Cisco White Paper, April 2011.

Fiolet, Elaine, "Kolibree Connected Electrical Toothbrush with 3D Motion Sensors," http://www.ubergizmo.com/2015/01/kolibree-connected-electrical-toothbrush-with-3d-motion-sensors/, January 6, 2015.

Goode, Lauren, "Intel Bets Its 'Smart' Shirt on the Future of Wearables," http://recode.net/2014/05/28/intel-bets-its-smart-shirt-on-the-future-of-wearables-video/, May 28, 2014.

Grove, Andrew S., Intel Keynote Transcript, Academy of Management Annual Meeting, August 9, 1998, San Diego, CA, http://www.intel.com/pressroom/archive/speeches/ag080998.htm.

Howells, Richard, "Are You Ready for the Internet of Everything?", *Forbes*, http://www.forbes.com/sites/sap/2014/07/09/are-you-ready-for-the-internet-of-everything/, July 9, 2014.

Jonnes, Jill. *Empires of Light: Edison, Tesla, Westinghouse, and the Race to Electrify the World*, New York: Random House, 2004.

Kastrenates, Jacob. "Apple's Homekit Turns the iPhone into a Remote for Your Smart Home," http://www.theverge.com/2014/6/2/5772158/iphone-homekit-smart-home-control-ios-8, June 2, 2014.

Kurzweil, Ray, "The Law of Accelerating Returns," http://www.kurzweilai.net/the-law-of-accelerating-returns, March 7, 2001.

Lackey, Mike, "How Will the 4th Industrial Revolution Affect Your Business?", http://sapinsider.wispubs.com/Assets/Articles/2014/July/SPI-how-will-the-4th-industrial-revolution-affect-your-business, July 1, 2014.

Laffler, Markus, and Andreas Tschiesner, "The Internet of Things and the Future of Manufacturing," http://www.mckinsey.com/insights/business_technology/the_internet_of_things_and_the_future_of_manufacturing, June 2013.

Leswing, Ki, "Apple's Healthkit Is Already Finding a Home in U.S. Hospitals," https://gigaom.com/2015/02/05/apple-healthkit-is-already-finding-a-home-in-u-s-hospitals/, February 5, 2015.

Mullooly, Morgan, "M2M DEVICE CONNECTIONS AND REVENUE: WORLDWIDE FORECAST 2013–2023," Analysys Mason, Research Report, http://www.analysysmason.com/Research/Content/Reports/M2M-connections-forecast-Aug2013_RDME0/, August 28, 2013.

Murray, Lance, "Sabre Holdings Sets IPO Valuation at up to $4.1B," http://www.bizjournals.com/dallas/news/2014/04/04/sabre-holdings-sets-ipo-valuation-at-up-to-4-1b.html, April 4, 2014.

Sager, Rebekah, "Tesla's Stocks Are Soaring," http://firsttoknow.com/teslas-stocks-are-soaring/, May 28, 2013.

Samsung BusinessVoice Team, "Tracking Everything Everywhere: How the Internet of Things Is Changing the Logistics Industry," *Forbes*, http://www.forbes.com/sites/samsungbusiness/2014/11/11/tracking-everything-everywhere-how-the-internet-of-things-is-changing-the-logistics-industry/, November 11, 2014.

Shankar, Udaya, "How the Internet of Things Impacts Supply Chains," http://www.inboundlogistics.com/cms/article/how-the-internet-of-things-impacts-supply-chains/.

Stawski, Scott, "Overcoming Disintermediation," http://www.destinationcrm.com/Articles/CRM-News/CRM-Featured-News/Overcoming-Disintermediation-45985.aspx, May 2, 2001.

Sullivan, Mark, "Proteus Digital Health Takes in Another $52 M for Med-Monitoring System," http://venturebeat.com/2014/07/29/proteus-digital-health-takes-in-another-52m-for-meds-monitoring-system/, July 29, 2014.

Tesla Motors, "Tesla Motors, Inc.—Fourth Quarter & Full Year 2014 Shareholder Letter," February 12, 2015.

Weinberg, Ari, "Will Orbitz's IPO Fly?" *Forbes*, http://www.forbes.com/2003/11/26/cx_aw_1126orbitz.html, November 26, 2003.

Wirth, Marco, and Frederic Thiesse, "Shapeways and the 3D Printing Revolution," Twenty-Second European Conference on Information Systems, Tel Aviv, 2014, http://ecis2014.eu/E-poster/files/0778-file1.pdfhttp://ecis2014.eu/E-poster/files/0778-file1.pdf.

Chapter 3

Hanft, Adam, "26 Most Fascinating Entrepreneurs," *Inc.*, http://www. inc.com/magazine/20050401/26-kurzweil.html, April 2005.

Hamel, Gary, and C. K. Prahalad, *Competing for the Future*, Boston: Harvard Business Press, 1996.

Johnson, Rod, "In a Crowded CRM Consultant Marketplace, Inforte Is One of the Few to Stand Out," *Gartner*, https://www.gartner.com/ doc/1346408/crowded-crm-consultant-marketplace-inforte, December 12, 2002.

Kurzweil, Ray, "The Law of Accelerating Returns," http://www. kurzweilai.net/the-law-of-accelerating-returns, March 7, 2001.

Pfeiffer, Eric W., "Start Up," *Forbes*, http://www.forbes.com/ asap/1998/0406/017_print.html, April 1998.

Porter, Michael E., *Competitive Advantage*, New York: The Free Press, 1985.

Prahalad, C. K., and Gary Hamel, "The Core Competence of the Corporation," *Harvard Business Review*, 68(3): 79–91.

Smith, Robert Norton. *The Colonel: The Life and Legend of Robert R. McCormick*, Boston: Houghton Mifflin, 1997.

Stawski, Scott, "Time for a New Model," *Editor & Publisher*, July 1, 2006.

"Who Made America? Ray Kurzweil," *PBS*, http://www.pbs.org/wgbh/ theymadeamerica/whomade/kurzweil_hi.html.

Chapter 4

"Del Monte tastes the fruits of business transformation," Hewlett Packard, Case Study, http://www8.hp.com/h20195/v2/GetDocument.aspx?docname=4AA5-8168ENW, June 2015.

DesMarais, Christina, "Facebook's Instagram Says It Has 90 Million Monthly Active Users," http://www.techhive.com/article/2025801/facebooks-instagram-says-it-has-90-million-monthly-active-users.html, January 20, 2013.

"Deutsche Bank and Hewlett-Packard sign agreement," Hewlett Packard, Press Release, February 24, 2015.

Gavin, Ted, "Top Five Reasons Why EBITDA Is a Great Big Lie," *Forbes*, http://www.forbes.com/sites/tedgavin/2011/12/28/top-five-reasons-why-ebitda-is-a-great-big-lie/, December 18, 2011.

Stumpp, Pamel M., Tom Marshella, Mike Rowan, Rob McCreary, Monica Coppola, "Putting EBITDA In Perspective: Ten Critical failings of EBITDA as the Principal Determinant of Cash Flow," Moody's Investor Service, http://www.ucema.edu.ar/u/jd/Inversiones/Articulos/Moodys_Putting_Ebitda_into_perspective.pdf, June 2000.

Chapter 5

Burton, Noel, *How to Manage the IT Helpdesk—A Guide for User Support and Call Center Managers*, London: Routledge Press, 2012.

Cearley, David W., "Gartner's Top 10 Strategic Technology Trends for 2015," *Gartner*, http://www.gartner.com/technology/research/top-10-technology-trends/, October 21, 2014.

Condon, Stephanie, "Dell Refused 'Cloud Computing' Trademark," *CNET Magazine*, http://www.cnet.com/news/dell-refused-cloud-computing-trademark/, August 18, 2008.

"Elasticity (Cloud Computing)," Wikipedia, http://en.wikipedia.org/wiki/Elasticity_%28cloud_computing%29.

Greiner, Lynn, "ABC: An Introduction to the IT Infrastructure Library," http://www.servicesphere.com/blog/2009/3/31/abc-an-introduction-to-the-it-infrastructure-library.html, March 31, 2009.

Martincic, Cynthia J., "A Brief History of ISO," http://www.sis.pitt.edu/~mbsclass/standards/martincic/isohistr.htm, February 20, 1997.

Mell, Peter, and Timothy Grance, "The NIST Definition of Cloud Computing," National Institute of Standards and Technology, Special Publication 800-145, http://csrc.nist.gov/publications/nistpubs/800-145/SP800-145.pdf, September 2011.

"P&G's Global Business Services: Transforming the way business is done," Proctor and Gamble, https://www.pg.com/en_US/downloads/company/PG_GBS_Factsheet.pdf. November 2010.

"Rising Use of Consumer Technology in the Workplace Forcing IT Departments to Respond, Accenture Research Finds," Accenture, News Release, https://newsroom.accenture.com/subjects/digital/rising-use-of-consumer-technology-in-the-workplace-forcing-it-departments-to-respond-accenture-research-finds.htm, December 12, 2011.

Regalado, Antonio, "Who Coined 'Cloud Computing'?" *MIT Technology Review*, http://www.technologyreview.com/news/425970/who-coined-cloud-computing/, October 31, 2011.

Segal, Leerom, "IT Policies Can Affect Recruiting and Retention," ERE Recruiting Intelligence, http://www.eremedia.com/ere/it-policies-can-affect-recruiting-and-retention/, February 20, 2014.

Weinzimer, Phil, "P&G's Filippo Passerini Stands Out as Stellar Example of a Strategic CIO," http://www.cio.com/article/2854239/cio-role/pandgs-filippo-passerini-stands-out-as-a-stellar-example-of-the-strategic-cio.html, December 3, 2014.

Chapter 6

Byrne, Tony, "Do You Need Mobile Middleware?", *Information-Week*, http://www.informationweek.com/it-leadership/do-you-need-mobile-middleware/d/d-id/1111717, September 27, 2013.

"Cisco Global Work Your Way Study for Mobility," Cisco, Research Study, http://www.cisco.com/c/en/us/solutions/enterprise-networks/unified-access/cisco_global_work.html, 2013.

"City engages HP to develop innovative mobile applications," Hewlett Packard, Case Study, http://businessvalueexchange.com/blog/2013/05/11/city-engages-hp-to-develop-innovative-mobile-applications/, 2012.

"Deputy UN chief calls for urgent action to tackle global sanitation crisis," United Nations, http://www.un.org/apps/news/story.asp?NewsID=44452#.VaT3svlViko, 2015.

"Gartner Predicts by 2017, Half of Employers will Require Employees to Supply Their Own Device for Work Purposes," *Gartner*, http://www.gartner.com/newsroom/id/2466615http://www.gartner.com/newsroom/id/2466615, May 1, 2013.

"Get connected. Next-generation enterprise: The future favours the connected," Hewlett Packard, White Paper, http://www8.hp.com/h20195/V2/getpdf.aspx/4AA4-7992EEW.pdf?ver=1.0, September 2013.

"Mobile Device Management," *Gartner*, http://www.gartner.com/it-glossary/mobile-device-management-mdm.

"Mobile Middleware," Tech Target/SearchSOA.com, http://searchsoa.techtarget.com/definition/mobile-middleware.

"Mobile Strategy," Xcube Labs, White Paper, http://www.xcubelabs.com/our-blog/white-papers/, 2013.

"Number of apps available in leading app stores as of May 2015," Statista, http://www.statista.com/statistics/276623/number-of-apps-available-in-leading-app-stores/, May 2015.

"Service-Oriented Architecture (SOA)," Tech Target/SearchSOA.com, http://searchsoa.techtarget.com/definition/service-oriented-architecture.

Thornhill, Ted, "Gone in 60 seconds: 168 million emails, 700,000 Google searches... a mind-boggling snapshot of what happens on the Internet in just ONE MINUTE," *Daily Mail*, http://www.dailymail.co.uk/sciencetech/article-2006091/Number-crunchers-just-happens-60-seconds-internet--A-LOT.html#ixzz3frkXJfUE, June 21, 2011.

Chapter 7

Apple Press Information, "Apple and IBM Forge Global Partnership to Transform Enterprise Mobility," https://www.apple.com/pr/library/2014/07/15Apple-and-IBM-Forge-Global-Partnership-to-Transform-Enterprise-Mobility.html, July 15, 2014.

"Four Reasons CIOs Should Still Hedge Their SaaS Bets," Forrester Research, White Paper, https://www.forrester.com/Four+Reasons+CIOs+Should+Still+Hedge+Their+SaaS+Bets/fulltext/-/E-RES119641, January 30, 2015.

"Gartner Says That by 2017, 25 Percent of Enterprises Will Have an Enterprise App Store," *Gartner*, http://www.gartner.com/newsroom/id/2334015http://www.gartner.com/newsroom/id/2334015, February 12, 2013.

Gilber, Alorie, "Rivals Vie for Siebel's Customer Spoils," *CNET Magazine*, http://news.cnet.com/Rivals-vie-for-Siebels-customer-spoils/2100-1017_3-959878.html, September 27, 2002.

"History of SAP AG," http://www.fundinguniverse.com/company-histories/sap-ag-history/.

Kepes, Ben, "Workday Posts Impressive Quarter and Announces a Tasty Acquisition," *Forbes*, http://www.forbes.com/sites/ben-kepes/2014/02/26/workday-posts-impressive-quarter-and-announces-a-tasty-acquisiton/, February 26, 2014.

Krill, Paul, "Open for Business: It's the Year of the Corporate App Store," Infoworld, http://www.infoworld.com/article/2616578/mobile-apps/open-for-business--it-s-the-year-of-the-corporate-app-store.html, April 16, 2012.

Paul, Gil, "What Is SaaS (Software as a Service)?", http://netforbeginners.about.com/od/s/f/what_is_SaaS_software_as_a_service.htm.

Rubino, Daniel, "UPS Mobile Launches Its Window Phone App," http://www.windowscentral.com/ups-mobile-launches-official-app-windows-phone, July 2, 2014.

Stead, Geoff, "Mobilize Your Learning with Employee App Stores," The Association for Talent Development, https://www.td.org/Publications/Magazines/TD/TD-Archive/2014/08/Mobilize-Your-Learning-with-Employee-App-Stores, August 8, 2014.

"Workday and Cardinal Health: Bringing Talent to the Top" Workday, Case Study, http://www.workday.com/Documents/pdf/case-studies/workday-cardinal-health-case-study.pdf, 2014.

Chapter 8

Bertolucci, Jeff, "5 Big Data Use Cases to Watch," http://www.informationweek.com/big-data/big-data-analytics/5-big-data-use-cases-to-watch/d/d-id/1251031, May 7, 2014.

"Big Data," *Oxford English Dictionary*, http://www. oxforddictionaries.com/us/definition/american_english/big-data.

Del Ray, Jason, "How Jeff Bezos Crushed Diapers.com so Amazon Could Buy Diapers.com," http://allthingsd.com/20131010/how-jeff-bezos-crushed-diapers-com-so-amazon-could-buy-diapers-com/, October 10, 2013.

Dormehl, Luke, "Amazon-Branded Diapers Are Pulled After Less Than Two Months on Sale," *Fast Company*, http://www.fastcompany.com/3041211/fast-feed/amazon-branded-diapers-are-pulled-after-less-than-two-months-on-sale, January 21, 2015.

Goldberg, Michael, "Inside the Obama Campaign's Big Data Analytics Culture," http://data-informed.com/inside-the-obama-campaigns-big-data-analytics-culture/, January 28, 2013.

Harris, Derrick, "A Real-Time Bonanza: Facebook's Wormhole and Yahoo's Streaming Hadoop," https://gigaom.com/2013/06/14/a-real-time-bonanza-facebooks-wormhole-and-yahoos-streaming-hadoop/, June 14, 2013.

King, Gary, "Big Data is Not About the Data!", http://gking.harvard.edu/files/gking/files/evbase-gs.pdf, January 30, 2013.

Press, Gil, "A Very Short History of Big Data," *Forbes*, http://www.forbes.com/sites/gilpress/2013/05/09/a-very-short-history-of-big-data/, May 9, 2013.

Press, Gil, "A Very Short History of the Internet of Things," *Forbes*, http://www.forbes.com/sites/gilpress/2014/06/18/a-very-short-history-of-the-internet-of-things/, June 18, 2014.

Williams, Paul, "A Short History of Data Warehousing," http://www.dataversity.net/a-short-history-of-data-warehousing/, August 23, 2012.

Woods, Dan. "Big Data Requires a Big, New Architecture," http://www.forbes.com/sites/ciocentral/2011/07/21/big-data-requires-a-big-new-architecture/, July 21, 2011.

Chapter 9

"A passion for research," IDC, Research Report, http://softwarestrategiesblog.com/category/idc/, 2013.

Barker, Colin. "Predicting the Future of the IT Department," http://www.zdnet.com/article/predicting-the-future-of-the-it-department/, April 22, 2014.

"By 2017 the CMO will Spend More on IT than the CIO," *Gartner*, White Paper, http://my.gartner.com/portal/server.pt%3Fopen%3D5 12%26objID%3D202%26mode%3D2%26PageID%3D5553%26ref %3Dwebinar-rss%26resId%3D1871515, 2012.

Conlin, Michelle, "Groupon's Fall to Earth Swifter Than Its Fast Rise," The Associated Press, http://news.yahoo.com/groupons-fall-earth-swifter-fast-rise-184713324.html, October 21, 2011.

"Get connected. Next-generation enterprise: The future favours the connected," Hewlett Packard, White Paper, http://www8.hp.com/h20195/V2/getpdf.aspx/4AA4-7992EEW.pdf?ver=1.0, 2013.

Gilson, Roland, and Mark J. Roe, "Understanding the Japanese Keiretsu: Overlaps Between Corporate Governance and Industrial Organization," *The Yale Law Journal*, 1993, 102: 871–906.

"Global Survey: What's Creating Tension Between IT and Business Leaders?" Avanade, Study, http://www.avanade.com/~/media/documents/resources/it-without-boundaries-global-study.pdf, April 2014.

"Seadrill makes rapid move from data center to cloud," Hewlett Packard, Case Study, video interview, http://www8.hp.com/h20621/video-gallery/us/en/sss/3391459850001/seadrill-makes-rapid-move-from-data-center-to-cloud--2-mins/video/, 2015.

Steiner, Christopher, "Meet the Fastest Growing Company Ever," *Forbes,* http://www.forbes.com/forbes/2010/0830/entrepreneurs-groupon-facebook-twitter-next-web-phenom.html, August 12, 2010.

Weiss, Barbi, "Groupon's $6 Billion Gambler," *The Wall Street Journal*, http://www.wsj.com/articles/SB1000142405274870482810457602 1481410635432, December 20, 2010.

"What Happened in 2008," http://www.thepeoplehistory.com/2008. html

Chapter 10

Tichy, Noel and Ram Charan, "Speed, Simplicity, Self-Confidence: An Interview with Jack Welch", *Harvard Business Review*, September 1989.

Wurtzel, Alan. *Good to Great to Gone: The 60 Year Rise and Fall of Circuit City*. New York: Diversion Publishing, 2012.

Index